HEAVEN'S MESSENGER

How an Ordinary Man Answered the Call from Above
to Fight Evil, Spread Light, and Deliver…
the Message

JARRED NEIL

Copyright © 2018 Jarred Neil

Published in Canada by Jarred Heaven's Messenger
All rights reserved.
Printed in the U.S.A.

No part of this book may be reproduced in any manner whatsoever without written permission from the author. All names have been changed to protect client confidentiality unless otherwise already published on
www.jarredheavensmessenger.com

Edited by Anne Shaughnessy
Cover design by Anne Shaughnessy

Back cover photo by Val Provost
Back cover logo © 2017 Jarred Heaven's Messenger
Front cover photo by Evan Shuster and Jeffrey de Belle

10 9 8 7 6 5 4 3 2 1

ISBN-13:
978-1-7753345-0-7

DEDICATION

This book is dedicated first and foremost to God. Without Him, I would have no gift and none of the blessings I have. I would also like to dedicate this book to my wife, Maya, who makes it possible for me to do what I do. Lastly, I want to dedicate this book to all those fighting for goodness and justice; all those spreading light and kindness, and fighting evil.

CONTENTS

	PREFACE	vii
	INTRODUCTION	xi
1	THE EARLY YEARS	1
2	BECOMING HEAVEN'S MESSENGER	10
3	WHAT DISTINGUISHES ME FROM THE REST?	17
4	GABRIEL MIKAEL	22
5	SKEPTICS, NON-BELIEVERS AND HATERS	27
6	IS WHAT I DO ACCEPTED IN SOCIETY?	37
7	BEING HEAVEN'S MESSENGER COMES WITH GREAT SACRIFICE	39
8	HAUNTED HOMES AND EXORCISMS	47
9	BEWARE THE WOLF IN SHEEP'S CLOTHING	53
10	FAKES, FRAUDS AND CON ARTISTS	58
11	THE NEW AGE MOVEMENT	67
12	SPIRIT STREET SMARTS	71
13	CLAIRVOYANT SESSIONS	78
14	CONTACT OF THE DECEASED SESSIONS	93

15	CLEARING HAUNTED HOMES	102
16	SHAMANIC SESSIONS	108
17	EXORCISMS	116
18	MESSAGES AND LESSONS WE CAN LEARN	130
19	FINAL THOUGHTS	134
	GLOSSARY OF SPIRITUAL DEFINITIONS	138
	TESTIMONIALS	143
	REFERENCES	157

JARRED NEIL

PREFACE

Julia was in trouble. No one could make sense of her odd behaviour, which was becoming increasingly erratic and alarming. On this night, Julia's antics had reached a critical point: She had threatened to kill her brother. Her eyes were pitch black, she was acting completely insane, and at one point, when it was Julia talking (and not the demonic entity inside her), she begged her mother and brother to get out of the house because she said she couldn't control this thing that was taking over her body. She feared what she would do to them. Julia's mother phoned me in a panic the following day, and I told her to bring Julia to me, and to not tell her where she was going.

Somehow, Julia's mother managed to find a way to get her to me. Unfortunately, when they arrived at my office, Julia didn't want to get out of the car. Since I need a person's permission to work on them, the situation now became even more difficult. I cannot go against someone's free will, so I need to ask for permission once they're of a certain age.

Luckily for all of us, I was able to get Julia's permission before the demon took over her body completely. I had to ask Julia several times if I had her permission to help her, and after a long while, she finally nodded yes. She had a blank stare, and at other moments, her eyes were jet black. Mostly though, she had a blank, deep stare where you could see nothing behind the eyes; staring like she was looking right through you. I could see that Julia was no longer in control of her body. She was mumbling and smirking, and I looked at her and said, "Don't worry, Julia. I'm going to help you." The 'thing' looked at me and answered back, "No, you can't help her," and I replied that my boss was strong enough that I could. It then looked at me and said, "My boss is stronger than yours," and proceeded to laugh. I simply replied, "You know that's not true. My boss is the strongest since he created the universe, and he created your boss."

We kept up this talk for a while, and during this time, we could see that Julia was pretty much gone. There was a tiny percentage of her left in her body, and most of the time I could hear the mumbling, and see the dark eyes, the smirk, and the blank stare.

It took me several hours to help her, but I was able to successfully kill the demon that was possessing her mind and body. I'm happy to report that Julia is back to her normal self and I am still in contact with this wonderful family. Julia did become Julia again!

What's particularly interesting about this story is that Julia's mother had noticed Julia texting someone in the car, while she was driving over to my office. Her mother asked who she was texting, and Julia said, "Just my friend." (The mother was able to get a screenshot of that text which she sent to me following the exorcism.). In the text conversation that ensued, Julia's friend could sense that something wasn't right with Julia, since it was not Julia who was texting, but rather the demon inside her, and her friend wrote, "I want to speak to Julia." The thing inside Julia answered, "I am that." Her friend clearly discerned that there was a problem because of that unusual response, and wrote, "I miss Julia." The thing inside Julia answered, "So come and see me." Her friend said, "When?" to which the thing inside Julia replied, "Before he comes to take me away."

The thing knew he was no match for me. It understood where it was going, who I was, and that I was going to win this battle. Julia's friend then replied, "Who is he?" and the thing answered, "Julia says it's Jared (sic)."

Once the exorcism was done, Julia's mother revealed to me a thought that she had on the drive over to my office. She was thinking about how she couldn't wait to get there so that I would mess up that demon and kill it. She was thinking, "Oh you demon, you scum, you have no idea what you're up against..."

The thing inside Julia knew what Julia's mother was thinking, and at that point, Julia grabbed her mother's shoulder and said, "I want to see the messages between you and Jarred." This all occurred without a word being uttered out loud.

I went to check on Julia and her mother a few days after the exorcism and saw entities in their house. While I stood in the doorway, I noticed that the dog refused to enter the hallway. I cleared the home and the dog was able to enter the hallway again.

Sounds like something right out of a Hollywood movie, doesn't it? But not only is this a true story with a happy ending, it's a typical account of the work I've been chosen to do.

INTRODUCTION

It's been an interesting and very busy last couple of years. My client base has grown exponentially to the point that I can proudly say I've helped people not only locally in Montreal, but throughout Canada and the U.S., Mexico, India, Nepal, Australia, France, England, Venezuela, the Philippines, Egypt, Morocco and Italy. Clients have flown me in to (or have been willing to visit me from) England, Dubai, New York, Los Angeles, Toronto, South Carolina, Texas and Jersey. I have received poignant pleas for help from people all over the world, but unfortunately, many have not had the means to bring me to their country or to visit me here in Canada.

The Heaven's Messenger video that I posted on social media not long ago quickly went viral, with over three million views to date, and counting.

I recently acted in a movie called The Lodge, filmed in Montreal, Quebec with a scheduled release date of November 2018. I would certainly love to do more acting and get much more involved in film and television. I am currently working on a few such projects.

For a humble guy like me, who enjoys the company of my family more than the spotlight, it has been, in some ways, a little overwhelming to be known and respected internationally, and to have such an impact on so many people. I am so grateful for the gift I have been chosen to have.

I felt the time was right to tell my story and share with you how I, an ordinary man with an extraordinary gift, can destroy demons, heal with just my hands, speak with deceased loved ones, and even see and predict life events. This isn't science fiction. It's very real, and by means of this book, I'll try and explain how this has all been made possible.

1

THE EARLY YEARS

I was a regular kid, just like all the other kids in the neighbourhood. In my younger years, I would spend my days and evenings playing wall ball in the schoolyard near my home, or playing street hockey or soccer baseball. I enjoyed sports and hanging out with my friends, and occasionally getting into some mischief, as most kids do. Times were different then. Parents didn't really worry about their kids being outside out of their view, because they knew we'd be home when it got dark. We always came home for dinner!

For a few years in high school, I hit the honour roll. I was a decent student, played on a few sport teams, and was involved in a few committees. My days were full and I was a popular kid. I managed to fit in everywhere I went. I got along with everyone. And that's the way that I wanted it.

But even at an early age, as far back as I can remember, I had experiences that I couldn't explain; experiences that I didn't tell my parents or my friends about, for fear that they would think I was crazy or that there was something wrong with me. I saw things others didn't. I felt things. I was able to hear and to speak to what I now know were entities. At the age of three or four, I understood that my imaginary friends were not really imaginary, but I didn't know what they were, these shadows, these visions of light, these forms of entities. I was also sensitive to the vibrations of people around me; there were people whom I instinctively did not like and others that I did, just based on the energy I felt around them.

As I got older, and I was able to verbalize a lot more what I was seeing, thinking, and feeling, I still kept most of it to myself, confiding in only a few friends. By the time I was a teenager, people started to hear that I had some 'supernatural abilities.' Word was spreading that I could see and predict things and feel energies. For fun, kids would bring me their girlfriend or boyfriend and ask me if they would be a good match, or ask me other questions of a psychic nature. My reward was simply a pat on the back, a handshake, or a couple of tokens for the arcade machine. I was still a regular guy, and most people had absolutely no clue about my growing abilities, including my family and most of my close friends.

Then, at the age of 18, I had my first encounter with a demon in human form; something of pure evil, up close and personal. It was the first time that I truly understood what was happening, and perhaps what was meant to come. I was at a party, and I went into a dark bathroom and took out a comb that I always carried with me. I wanted to look good for some of the girls that were at the party. As I walked into this dark room, I came face to face with someone I knew very well. She was part of our gang, so to speak; kids that we hung around with almost every day. She was a stunningly gorgeous girl, with beautiful red hair, blue eyes, and white satiny skin. She was quite the sweet talker too. Every single guy in our group of 20 or so kids fell head over heels in love with her. And I know how she did it. She slept with each one and then broke their heart. I was the only one who hadn't fallen for her charms. Never really knowing why, I found my answer that night. Here we were now, face to face in this room, and I looked her in the eyes, and at that very moment, I understood who, or rather what, she was. I didn't see a soul. She was a demon in human form. She noticed that I had come to this realization, and she threw her head back, laughed, and said, "So, you finally know what I am. That's OK. You are the only one that I couldn't get and I know why. You'll also know why when you're older. You'll know exactly who you are. But it's OK. It doesn't matter who you are or who you work for, because my side will win this battle. Not your side." And it was one of the last times I ever saw her, as shortly after, she moved away. I never heard from her again.

Many people assume that when a child has a divine gift, it's passed down from their parents, and that other siblings might have it; and that it then gets passed down from generation to generation. This is not how it works. My parents had no such spiritual gift, nor did my brother, or my grandparents. It's interesting to note though, that all five of my children have a gift to varying degrees, but it has nothing to do with me. It's who they are, and their spiritual gifts were given to them to help me here on earth. This is why they all have a gift. Even my wife Maya has a gift to a certain degree. It isn't at my level but she clearly has spiritual ability.

When I was a teenager, I had no idea that the gift I was blessed with would change my life forever. Back then, it did not feel that way. Sometimes it was fun and interesting, but for the most part, it felt more like a nuisance than anything else.

I grew up in a regular family. We grew up Jewish, but not religious. A middle class family, we had what we needed and we even had a little bit of what we wanted. We grew up on the outskirts of Montreal, in the suburbs. It was a nice little area. We had a decent life. A lot of kids had more than we did, but many had less. My brother and I went to a regular school, like everybody else. In many ways, I was just your average kid. Even though I had this gift, and even though I understood that I was different from others because of it, it didn't change me, and it didn't affect me. Maybe that's because I didn't understand what it really was or what I was meant to do with it.

My guardian angel, who happens to be archangel Mikha'el (most people know him by the name Michael, but I call him by his Hebrew name), played a very significant role in preventing bad things from happening to me - even saving my life - many times during my young adult years. I can recall many intense and crazy experiences back then that I now know was archangel Mikha'el intervening to help me.

One such time was on a trip to Venezuela. I was in my early twenties, and I was spending time with friends at a popular club on the island of Margarita when it was raided by what I found out later was the secret police division of the Venezuelan military. At that time, they were looking for drug dealers and they began separating the locals from the tourists. Anyone who wasn't moving fast enough was getting hit with a rifle butt.

A military truck was waiting, and people were being thrown in the truck. They were in search of foreigners, not locals, and anyone who didn't have their passport or identification as to why they were there, was being thrown in the back of the truck.

I knew enough about world events at that time to realize that in certain countries, when you get thrown in the back of a military vehicle, sometimes no one sees or hears from you again. I began to panic, because this was one of the first times in my life that I didn't have ID or a passport on me. I had had quite a few drinks at the club and was inebriated, having a good time with a couple of my Venezuelan friends. As the military police were interrogating everyone, I noticed that there were people crying on the other side of the road, and this wasn't giving me very much hope.

It came my turn, and luckily at that time, I spoke Spanish almost fluently. A man wearing a ski mask, who had four stars on his shoulders, looked at me and said, "Passport or papers (in Spanish). Believe me when I say that I sobered up pretty quick, and I looked at him and said, "Excuse me, sir (all in Spanish of course), please, do you mind if I say something?" And even though he was wearing this ski mask, I could see his eyebrows go up as if to say, "Who is this gringo, this non-Latino speaking to me in Spanish?", and he nodded for me to go ahead and I said, "Sir, I'm so sorry. I don't have my papers with me. I normally do. I'm staying at a hotel about a 10-minute walk from here and I'd be willing to run there to get you my passport to show you who I am and to show you that I'm a Canadian citizen. And I pointed at my friends across the street who were crying and said, "As you can see, they are very concerned for me. I speak the language, I love this country, I'm here because I do, and I love the culture and the people. Please sir, give me an opportunity. I'm just here to have a good time and enjoy the people, and your culture, and your country. I will get you the passport. Please allow me to run to the hotel." He asked me how old I was, and I said, "Sir, I'm 21." And he told me, "My son is 21." Then he said to me in Spanish, "Kid, you have balls. Most people would have been shot just for speaking to me without my permission."

He continued, "You obviously took the time to learn my language and a little bit about my culture which I respect very much, so I'm going to turn around, and

I'm going to count to 10, and you run. And as long as I don't see you when I turn around, I'll pretend that I never did." Let me tell you that was the fastest I've ever run in my entire life!

At about the same age, I was visiting Egypt with friends. We decided to ride horses in the middle of the desert. We started off at the pyramids in Giza, Cairo. It had been a long day and I had enjoyed some of the local 'flavours' which put me in a very nice state of mind. I ended up falling asleep on the horse. When I woke up, it was pitch black, and I was all by myself in the middle of the desert, on this horse. I had no clue where I was, I had no food or water with me, and none of my friends were with me. It was a terrifying experience, and I was sure that I was going to die. I passed out again, and when I woke up once more, I found myself exactly where I had started out with the horse, right at the base of the pyramids, in Giza. My friends were there, waiting for me. Archangel Mikha'el saved my life again. He confirmed this to me.

These are just two of the many unexplainable instances where I managed to dodge a bullet.

There were at least six or seven times when something or someone prevented me from being injured or even killed. It would happen when I was driving and was stopped at a red light. When the light turned green for me to go, I felt something hold me back. Sometimes people even honked behind me, but still, I didn't move. And at that very moment, a car would go right through a red light. If I had started to drive when my light had turned green, I would have been hit, at full speed, by an oncoming car, becoming gravely injured or killed.

Another time in Egypt, part of a building collapsed only a few feet from where we had been standing just a few seconds previously. It might have been a terrorist attack; to this day, officials have not confirmed what happened.

In 2000, I was in Israel, which I refer to as the Holy Land, and there were talks of peace; real talks of peace. People on both sides were hopeful. For Israelis and Palestinians, there was a sense that there would be an agreement, a deal. But I knew better. While I was there, I smelled it in the air. I felt it. And even when I would tell soldiers, "Tell your commanders to tell the government that war is coming soon. I feel it. Not next year, but maybe next week or the week after. It's coming very soon, maybe even tomorrow," the soldiers would laugh at me. They would say, "The newspapers are talking about peace on both sides. The radio, the foreign media, CNN, BBC, Fox News - they're all talking about peace. All the heads of government are saying that peace is coming to the Middle East." And I told everyone, "It is not."

Sure enough, three weeks later, war broke out and there were many casualties, unfortunately, on both sides. Many innocent people were killed. It was one of those times where I wished I had been wrong. I

HEAVEN'S MESSENGER

wished that my gut feeling, my intuition, and the war I saw in my mind had been wrong.

2

BECOMING HEAVEN'S MESSENGER

Things started to intensify as I got older. As the months and years passed, I could feel that I was meant to do something important. Something big. I almost felt as if I had the weight of the world on my shoulders. I actually felt a heaviness on my shoulders!

The need to investigate this 'gift' that I had grew stronger. My sixth sense began to deepen and I was able to experience things much more profoundly, gaining a heightened awareness of the energies around me. Even though I did not understand what the gift was or all that it would entail, or even what I was meant to do with it, I knew that there was much more to this that needed to be investigated. So one day, I turned to Maya and said, "I need to figure this out, and now. It is an overwhelming feeling. I can't keep going like this." And of course, she agreed.

Eventually I got the name and number of a man named Daniel, and after doing some research and reflection, I called him. A gentleman in his 60s, he had been a medium, psychic, and shaman (medicine man), for about 35 years.

I was indeed lucky that he picked up the phone. He spoke French and said "Allo." Without giving him my name, I said, "I'm calling you because I have some type of gift. I'm not sure what it is, although I'm sure it isn't going to be anything like the gift that you have, but..." He interrupted me and said, "How do you know it's not going to be like what I have? In fact, I can tell you right now that within two years, it will be much bigger and stronger than anything I've ever been able to do in 35 years. You are the Hebrew I've been waiting for." This caught me completely off guard. I was surprised and overwhelmed by these words, and I asked him, "I haven't even told you my name. My name is Jarred. It's not a Hebrew name. How could you possibly know that I'm Jewish and why were you waiting for my call?" He came straight to the point. "Jarred, the angels who guide me from above (and who will be some of the same angels to guide you), told me to expect a call from a very powerful soul - someone who is going to have an extraordinary gift. One of the most powerful gifts that has ever been seen. And I knew that it was you, because only a Hebrew can have this power that I can sense from you as we speak."

He continued, "I am not a Hebrew, but the angels all have Hebrew names for a reason. And there is a reason that Moses and Abraham and King David and King Solomon, and Jesus, Mary and Joseph, and all 12 disciples were all Hebrews. There is a power that comes from being a Hebrew that cannot be found anywhere else."

I was astounded. Here I was, calling Daniel to understand what gift I had and how to properly use it, and he was bombarding me with this revelation. I now realized that he was the one who was going to help me understand what kind of gift I had and what I was supposed to do with it. Needless to say, by the time I had taken my appointment and hung up the phone, I now felt that it was the universe that I carried on my shoulders - not just the world!

A few weeks later, I finally met Daniel at his home, an hour outside of Montreal. A short, round gentleman with glasses, he had a kind face, and a kind aura about him. He spoke only French, and I learned that his grandfather was a native shaman, making Daniel part native. His home was a reflection of his travels, with artifacts from around the world that he had collected over the years. He also had many Hebrew artifacts and texts which I found interesting. Incense was burning, and candles were lit. As I sat down with pen and paper in hand, he began to tell me that I was different from anyone he had ever met, and was at a level he had never seen.

We began to have a very long conversation; a very deep, intense, fascinating one, and it became very clear to me what my gift entailed, what I was meant to do with it and how I was to go about doing so. It's one thing to have a gift; now I needed to learn how to use it and develop it properly. Over several months, I spent a lot of time with Daniel; he had a wealth of experience, and I learned so much from him. He helped me to understand, develop and use the gift that was handed to me from above, to the best of my ability, so that I could help as many people as possible.

Once my lessons with Daniel were done, I understood that I was now Heaven's Messenger. I understood the big responsibilities that came with being Heaven's Messenger. The sacrifices that would be required. The joys, the heartbreaks, and the energy that would need to be sustained to be able to carry out these responsibilities.

I had a choice. I didn't have to accept this role, but I chose to, because I understood that this was what I was born to do. I had this gift, given to me from heaven no less, and it was not to be dismissed or put aside. All of my life up to this point, I had simply been waiting for the right opportunity to use this gift to its fullest potential.

To be honest, once I understood the magnitude of what being Heaven's Messenger was all about, I was overcome with emotion. Many things raced through my mind. "Why am I so blessed to be chosen to do this? Why do I deserve this honour and privilege and blessing?" It was emotionally overwhelming, and many years later, I still occasionally ask myself, "Why me?" At the moment that I accepted this responsibility, I accepted who I was, who I was to become, and what I needed to do. It's a responsibility that has grown steadily each passing year.

I was born with an extraordinary gift, one that I feel privileged to have, and one that I realize must be used in the pursuit of helping others. Whether it's helping someone find solace after a loved one passes on, helping someone to make better business or personal decisions, or other life-changing decisions, I can and want to help. Being able to help give people their health back when traditional medicine has failed to do so, or restoring calm and peace in someone's home after weeks or months of unexplainable terror or confusion, I can help people get back on their feet. It's an honour to be bestowed this gift, and I want to use it to make a positive difference in people's lives.

I am blessed to be able to offer my services through the power of the eight archangels, Jesus and a few holy souls with whom I work. I am a vessel for their light. Only with their help can I help others. Without them, I have no gift.

My life's mission, now and always, is to help as many people as I can, which is the reason that I wrote this book. I want to give people options, to know where to turn, and know what to do in times of despair, chaos or uncertainty. Perhaps now, they will know.

I have already foreseen what I will do, who I will be, and how my life will change down the road, 5, 10 and 20 years from now. Some of my future plans cannot be discussed at this time, however, I do plan on writing several more books about my life and about what I do, and the spiritual world in general.

My biggest wish is to travel more to be able to help people around the world. But for now, my mission is to help as many people as I can, one by one, regardless of their background, colour, creed, race, religion, nationality or sexual orientation. We are all human, and we are all inherently good people. I want to help those who are open to my help; I can't help those who are not. Maybe they are sick, or need guidance; maybe they seek closure after losing a loved one. Perhaps their home is haunted, or a family member or friend is possessed or being bothered by a demon. People come and see me for so many different reasons.

Part of my mission is also to educate. I get the opportunity when I meet people, to chat with them, to find out who they are, where they come from, and what they're all about, and they get to find out the same from me. I want to open people's minds as to what truly is out there, and to also let them know that perhaps they shouldn't believe everything they're being told; that we should question everything. That perhaps we should do our own research - not simply be zombies and sheep, going along with what everybody else says or does. Every person that I meet, every person that I help, gives me an opportunity to open their mind and answer some of the questions they may have.

The biggest part of my mission, whether I'm helping them or sharing an opinion, is making a difference for every person that I meet. I want to help them and change their life in a positive way; to give them a helping hand, a guiding hand, a pat on the back, whatever it is they need. While I'm doing this, I'm also fulfilling my mission of spreading the light of heaven, of spreading goodness and kindness. For every person that I help, I'm fighting the shadow. I'm pushing it back. For me, it doesn't get better than that.

3

WHAT DISTINGUISHES ME FROM THE REST?

My blessings in life are numerous. I'm a father, a husband, and friend to many. I'm just a regular guy with an extraordinary gift. In the spiritual industry, you can find mediums, clairvoyants, and to a lesser extent, shamans (medicine person). You are much less likely to find a haunted house specialist or an exorcist. What separates me from others in the spiritual field is that I am all of these.

I was also born with this gift, and in my humble and professional opinion, to work in the light, you must be born with this gift. You can't take a course to learn to do what I do. You can't take a course on how to be a shaman, or to learn how to speak to angels, or speak to the deceased. You can't take a course on how to play around with energy, or how to fight and destroy demons. You either have it, or you don't. And if you don't, and you wake up one day and say to yourself that you'd love to acquire some of these supernatural abilities, you may end up getting a modest ability after learning more about your chosen field, but trust me when I say, it's not coming from the light; it's coming from the shadow.

Approximately 5% of people claim to have some type of psychic ability. Of this small group, only one of those five actually works in the light, not the shadow. Works with heaven, as opposed to hell. Works with good, as opposed to evil. And of the four who work with the shadow, I want to be very clear: Half of them know that they're working with the shadow and do so because they get fame, money and power. The other half working in the shadow don't even know it. They think they're working in the light. And that's where these four out of 100 people who have a 'gift' come in. These people take a course to acquire spiritual abilities; they are not born with this gift.

To recap, one out of every 100 people claiming to have some type of spiritual gift works in the light as opposed to the shadow. Being in this tiny percentage of those who have a genuine, divine gift, makes me unique. (The above synopsis is simply my opinion, as statistics are not readily available for this type of information, however, in my years of experience and familiarity with the subject, I believe this to be a fairly accurate assumption.).

To break it down even further, among people who have a legitimate gift, most have only one or two specialties: maybe they're clairvoyant and can see the future, maybe they have mediumistic abilities and can speak to spirits or the deceased in some way, shape or form, on a small level - perhaps they can do both. Maybe someone is a shaman who helps people who are sick. This is certainly possible. But usually, they're able to do one, maybe two or three things. My gift, being a messenger for above and being born with my gift, allows me to do all of the above as well as being a haunted house specialist and exorcist.

There are very few people worldwide, out of 7.3 billion people, who can offer many services with their spiritual gift. My gift simply allows me to become a vessel for heaven, and allows me to do all of the above.

I don't know exactly how many people can actually walk into a haunted house and get rid of entities with only their hands. There are very few of us, perhaps 10-15 people worldwide who are working with the light, who can perform actual and legitimate exorcisms, and can walk into a home and clear the entities and demons and ghosts just with their hands, as I can.

I feel it's important to mention that I don't consider myself better or more "special" than others. Without heaven, I have no gift at all, and I can't help anyone. Through Jesus and the archangels, I am able to do all of this. I work closely with Jesus, whom I call by His Hebrew name, Yeshua. He was known as a healer. He was also known as someone who fought demons. Since part of what I do and what my mission entails is to fight demons and help those who suffer physically, it makes sense to work with the one most known for that since the beginning of time! Jesus helps me with this and more. Much more. I speak with Him daily. Anyone working in the light must work with Jesus; otherwise, they are not truly working in the light.

I am also a stigmatic. Stigmata is used to describe body marks, sores, or sensations of pain in the hands, wrists and feet; the same marks as those of Jesus Christ on the Cross. In every generation, there are only a handful of people who are proven to potentially have the stigmata. I'm one of the very few right now who actually suffers the stigmata. My wife, Maya, is another, as she and I are so connected, that she simply feels what I do, much like an echo after the first sound. From what I am able to gather, there are maybe only five or six people in the world who experience this. Some people have seen the holes in my hands and feet; some people have seen the marks that occasionally manifest. I will speak to this subject in more depth later in this book.

Finally, my being a Hebrew puts me in a different category from the rest. There are very few, at my level, who are from the Hebrew tribe. Jesus was also Hebrew, and this is one of the deep and powerful reasons why I am connected to Jesus. One day, I will reveal who I was and how I was connected to Jesus on a deeper level.

My kids also possess a gift similar to mine. As my children get older, they will be able to manifest and become Messengers of Heaven as well. Some will be stronger in certain aspects of their gift than others, but all five of my children have a spiritual gift. Their gift was not handed down from me; our children were sent to Maya and I from a high level and are meant to do what I do. Anyone who has met my children has sensed and seen that they are different, filled with light. I am so blessed to have five gifted children!

4

GABRIEL MIKAEL

After having four beautiful children, Maya and I decided that our family was complete. Our fourth child, a daughter, is named Eliana. In Hebrew, Eliana means God has answered our prayer. On my father's side of the family, there has only been one girl born in the last 100+ years. Our daughter is the second one. So with three boys and one girl, Maya and I decided that we were done, and I made an appointment for a vasectomy. I then got a message from above, saying "Hold on, don't go to that appointment just yet."

At this point in time, it was physically, emotionally and financially draining to be raising four young children, so I said, "OK guys, if the Big Boss wants us to have another child, Maya and I will, absolutely, but I need a little bit to go on here." I got my answer through visions from above. I cancelled my appointment. Not long after, Maya and I were intimate, and almost immediately after, our bedroom was immersed in an intense white light that I had seen before; one that only comes from the Creator. There is no light that bright, that special and holy, on earth. This intense light filled up the room for about ten seconds, then faded away. My guardian angel, Mikha'el (known as Michael to most people) came, and I witnessed him bringing a soul and placing it inside my wife. It all happened so quickly. For anyone who thinks it takes days, weeks or months for there to be a life form, I can tell you emphatically, it happens in less than a minute. That soul was inside my wife almost instantly. Maya began to cry; I looked at her and asked, "Why are you crying?" She said, "Something just happened." "Well, you're pregnant," I said. Needless to say, she was!

About a month into the pregnancy, I happened to be in a deep meditation, when the angels with whom I speak told me that the Big Boss, the Creator, wanted to speak to me. Now, I don't know how many people throughout time have had the privilege, honour or absolute blessing to speak to God, but it's a feeling, or experience which cannot be put into words. I said, "Me? The Big Boss wants to speak to me?" And they said, "Yes."

I started getting this feeling of an intense light enveloping my entire body, and I received the message, "I want to thank you and Maya. Throughout your life, you've had many reasons to doubt my existence. Many things have happened where most people would have given up on Me, and you never did. And here is another example of how you didn't want to have another child; and yet I asked. And as soon as you knew that's what I wanted, you were decided. I want to thank you, and to let you know that this child is holier than you can possibly imagine. This child will bring you blessings you cannot even dream of. I am going to make sure of that. I want to thank you and tell you this: Somebody wants to speak to you now." And then I heard, in my head, "Abba," which is Hebrew for father, "It's me, Abba." I was approximately one hour away from my family, so I knew it wasn't one of my four children calling me. Then it hit me. The tears started to flow down my cheeks, as I realized just who was talking to me. The voice continued, "Yes, Abba, I'm talking to you from mama's belly. It's me. And I will bring you and mama many, many blessings. I want to thank you for the decision to have me."

This experience was so emotional for me, it was mind-boggling. And the baby said, "Don't worry about finding a name. When the time is right, before I am born, I will tell you and mama what my name is." And indeed, he did. About two months before he was born, he told us his name would be Gabriel Mikael. He explained it was because he was very close with the two archangels of the same name. For the entire nine-month pregnancy, I was able to speak with Gabriel Mikael, and it was a truly extraordinary experience.

For the first time in Maya's five pregnancies, during her labor, her water didn't break. Two doctors tried on three different occasions to break the water, but were unsuccessful. They kept trying, as labor is more difficult and more painful when the water isn't broken, and during this time, I happened to remember something I had seen just recently. Archangel Mikha'el had appeared inside my wife's body and I saw him doing something with his hands. I asked him, "What are you doing?" And he replied, "Don't worry about it. He will be OK. He is one of ours, and we will take care of him." The doctor's attempts at rupturing the amniotic sac were futile, and they just couldn't understand why the water wouldn't break. They both admitted that they had never witnessed this before, the fact that they couldn't at least make a dent or create a little break in the amniotic sac, to start the labor.

On the second push, the baby came out and was dragged back in, at which point, Maya gave another big push and the baby started to emerge again. The doctors were panicking at this point because they could see that the cord was wrapped around the baby's neck, not once, not twice, but three times. The doctors began to suspect that the baby was dead or severely injured, maybe brain damaged or having some other injury that would have lasting effects. They proceeded to take the cord off of his neck, and to everyone's surprise, there wasn't even a mark on his skin! The baby was perfectly fine, perfectly healthy. Archangel Mikh'ael came to me at this point, and said, "I will now explain to you what I did. We knew that the cord was wrapped around his neck three times, and had the water broken, the baby would have come out faster after your wife pushed, and the cord would have snapped his neck. It would have killed him. What you saw me doing was putting a shield of light around the water, which is why the doctors couldn't break the water. It enabled the baby to come out slower, giving the doctors the opportunity to take the cord off the baby's neck."

At the time of this writing, Gabriel Mikael is three years old, and he has brought us many blessings. Certainly, anyone who has met him can see that he is not a regular child, by the things he says and does. Although Maya and I love all five of our children the same, and every child has a special gift to a different degree, it's apparent that Gabriel Mikael may be at a higher spiritual level than the others.

5

SKEPTICS, NON-BELIEVERS AND HATERS

I cannot help everyone. The Creator gave all of us free will, or free choice, which is why in anything I do, I never tell anyone that they cannot do this, or that they must do this. I simply offer my guidance, or messages passed on to me from above, and then let people make their own decisions. I can only help those who allow me to help them.

For example, someone who is sick may come and see me, and the angels will tell me that I can help save them. But if the sick person doesn't have faith in my methods, then I cannot help them. Someone who may be possessed, but says they don't believe in what I do; unfortunately, I can't help them. When a parent contacts me and says, "My 18-year-old child is possessed," but this child doesn't believe this is true, doesn't believe in my gift and won't allow me to help; I can't do anything for this person because I am not allowed to go against someone's free will. I have no right to go against someone's personal choices, or free will. Even if it means helping someone, I cannot do so unless the person allows me to. It is wrong to take away someone's free choice and free will. The Creator gave each of us the ability to make choices. That's what allows us to choose between doing good and doing evil. How can I remove what was given by the Lord? The angels would never help me do so anyway.

In my day-to-day interactions with people, I encounter four types of folks: skeptics, non-believers, haters, and believers. For non-believers and haters, I unfortunately cannot help them.

Someone who is a complete non-believer is someone who is close-minded. I don't judge people, but I don't understand non-believers. You don't get very far in life when you have a closed mind. There are things we don't understand, things that we do not know, things we can learn every single day; and someone who is close-minded is limiting their knowledge of who they can become, and how much they can grow as a person. They are limiting themselves so much. They are putting themselves in a box and closing the lid. I unfortunately cannot help non-believers. I won't even waste my time because I'm not here to change their mind if they don't believe in what I do, or if they think this is all impossible. I'm here to help those who want help.

For those who don't believe, they would be wasting their money coming to see me. It's also much more difficult for spirits to come through to those who are not open to receiving messages. And for me, it's not about time or money, it's about making a difference for someone. A non-believer will never believe that they are wrong. Which brings me to haters: There's a very fine line sometimes between non-believers and what I call haters. Some people are just brought up in certain ways, whether it's by organized religion, their parents' influence, or by their surroundings or environment. As human beings, we are brought up in a certain way where we are either brainwashed or put into a box, where the focus is wanting us to believe what others want us to believe. We become who we are because of the influence of our family, the school system, the media, entertainment, our neighbourhood, our friends, religious organizations, and our environment. As human beings, our thoughts and belief system are completely influenced by outside sources. This is where it becomes important to be open-minded - to go beyond the outside influences that have shaped our beliefs and our opinions.

Anyone who is reading this and is honest with themselves should be able to admit that their opinions and their belief systems have been shaped by outside influences and organizations, and by others, and that very often, the only way to find out who we are, and what we're meant to do and become, is to go outside that belief system. Outside what we've been taught to believe; outside the influences that have shaped what we think to be true.

We need to break free of these influences sometimes, to find out the truth, to discover who we are as individuals, as souls, who are here to grow. I don't condemn non-believers because, in most cases, it's not their fault, because of how our minds, our emotions and our belief systems are shaped by these outside influences.

What's important to understand in all of this is because of this, very often, these people develop hate. And there are those who hate me for what I do. Those working with darkness, those working with demons certainly hate what I do because I'm a good person, I'm a kind person, I make a positive difference for people and I spread the light. The shadow certainly hates me. Darkness doesn't like when the light is spread. Certain individuals will hate me because I speak the truth and it goes against their beliefs; what they believe to be true, and unshakable. To them, what I am able to do is heresy, and because of this, I must be a bad person. They're thinking, how dare I question their belief system or say something that they know cannot possibly be true. Some people will hate me because their religious authority will tell them that they should despise and turn their back on somebody like me, in the same way that some religious authorities will tell people that they should hate gays, or abhor people who commit suicide, that they should hate people of certain colour, certain backgrounds, ethnicities or religions.

Many of my clients ask me how I react to those who hate, and I tell them that I won't have a conversation with somebody who hates me. What good would this do? I'm not going to change their minds, and I'm simply going to get frustrated. As I've mentioned previously, I would rather devote my time and energy to someone who wants help and for whom I can make a difference. There are always going to be haters. When you're successful, there are always going to be people who hate you out of jealousy, or because you're different. They're going to hate you for many reasons, so there's no point in focusing on it. And I won't get angry at those who hate; the issue is with them, not with me. Maybe they hate themselves, maybe they hate where they are in life. Maybe they know that everything that they've been taught is false, and hearing some other ideas is too much for them to handle.

Skeptics are a different story, however. I love skeptics. These people are not sure if they believe. They may not, but they are still open-minded to the concept. Someone who is skeptical still leaves the door open to the possibility that they could be wrong; that what I do could be possible. They choose to think that maybe, just maybe, I can help them. Some of my biggest supporters, some of my best clients, some of the people who have referred me to others, were very skeptical. Because they were open-minded, and they were open to the possibility that they could be wrong - that I could be real - they now believe. That's why when someone is a skeptic, even a big skeptic, and I'm able to show them what I can do, and can prove that I can actually make a difference for them - when I can do what they never thought was possible for anyone to do - they become very, very big supporters. When someone has their mind blown because they weren't expecting something to be real, and they realize it is real, it becomes a very powerful, profound and emotional experience. I'm proud to say that I've amazed even the unwavering skeptics.

So, with skeptics, non-believers and haters, I will focus only on the skeptics. I'm not here to prove anything to anybody. I'm here to help those who are open-minded enough to seek my help and to give it a chance. People who believe that there is something that they may not know or understand. People who are open to the idea that there is something bigger and greater than all of us.

And finally, why are clients sometimes hesitant to see me, even when they believe in what I do, or possess an open mind? Sometimes, these people even know someone who has been satisfied with a service they've received from me. Whether it be for a clairvoyant session, a haunted house, to contact a deceased loved one – whatever the reason – sometimes people change their mind and decide not to follow through. Is it because they don't like me or my approach, how I work, or is it the cost? Maybe. But most of the time, it's none of the above. I have helped many people who needed a service but didn't have the money, offering my service for free or at a reduced fee.

Even people who have actually sat down in front of me and explained their situation, decide to back out. Many people refuse to accept what they know deep down to be true. They don't want to get out of their comfort zone. They prefer to stay in a box. They have been brought up a certain way, with certain belief systems that they abide by their entire life; they believe what the education system has taught them, what their parents have taught them, what they've seen in the media. Society tends to put people in a box and assign a label. These people are comfortable in their box. How many times have you heard about people too scared to make changes, even when things aren't going the way they want them to go? They prefer having less success in order to stay in their comfort zone. Many prefer to stay in this bubble, to not know what's going on around them, to not know the evil that's going on around the world. These people will say to me, "Listen, I know you're the real deal, that you'll tell me not just what I want to know, but what I need to know. And I know that even if it's negative, it's still good for me to know, but I would just rather not know at this time." I hear this all the time! They would rather not hear the truth, for fear it will create a change in their life that they're not ready to accept.

I once had a parent with a possessed 5-year-old child in my office, and she proceeded to tell me that the child had picked her up and thrown her across the room with one hand. I could see the child's eyes were black and he was speaking in foreign tongue right in front of me. Doctors might have told the mother that her child had schizophrenia or some other mental illness. Of course, that wouldn't explain the superhuman strength the child possessed, but people will come up with every possible excuse before they believe that something otherwordly could be going on. So this parent said to me, "I believe in what you do; I believe it's possible that my son is possessed. I believe that you can probably help him, but we're not going ahead with this."

Most people have been taught that the supernatural world is nonsense, that people cannot be possessed. If they were to see with their own eyes that their child was better after an exorcism, it would challenge their entire belief system. How many people believe that God doesn't exist, or that angels and demons don't exist? How many people deny the existence of spirits or the afterlife? For someone who has spent their entire life believing these things to be false, it now forces them to see that everything they've believed in the past has not been true. And if this isn't true, what else might they have believed that isn't true? It takes them way out of their box.

Can we prove that there's an afterlife, that there are different spirits around us, that there's a God? Just because there isn't a mathematical formula or other scientific explanation to prove these things, doesn't mean they don't exist.

Here are two more examples of severe cases in which people contacted me and decided not to use my services. One client called me and told me that she and her husband thought there was an entity in their home and proceeded to tell me the strange things that were going on. They had a newborn baby who was not yet able to roll over or crawl, and yet, when they placed the baby on one side of the crib, they would notice that the baby was on the other side of the crib when they checked up on him a few minutes later. They were in shock, as they told me they could watch the baby all day and the baby would not move. How could the baby get from one side of the crib to the other? It seemed impossible. They decided to install a video camera, and according to the parents, they could clearly see an entity, a shadow moving around the room. It was very clear that something non-human was moving the baby in the crib.

As a parent, it doesn't matter what your belief system is, you do everything in your power to ensure your children are safe. So why did this person decide not to use my services? Her husband didn't believe in what I do. The evidence was right in front of him, in black and white, but because he didn't believe in ghosts or spirits, it must have been all in their imagination! There must be some scientific explanation! Because of her husband's beliefs, she couldn't have me come over to their house. She knew enough to contact me because of what she saw in the video, but she had to decline because her husband didn't believe!

This, in my expert opinion, put the newborn baby in danger. I even told her, "What if one day, this thing picks up the baby, and decides to drop him on his head outside of the crib? How are you going to feel then?" I admit that I was that blunt, but it was too much for them to get out of their comfort zone and rectify this situation immediately. To this day, I'm haunted by this situation and pray for this baby.

The second example relates to a shamanic session. Now I'm very clear that I am a vessel for heaven. Without help from above, I have no ability to help someone. When someone who is sick with disease or in pain comes to see me, I'm honest with them. Sometimes it works and sometimes it doesn't. Sometimes it works 100% and sometimes it works 50% or less. It depends on the situation, but I have helped many people with many different issues.

A sick child was brought to me one day, and this child's health was deteriorating. Doctors had not been able to figure out what was wrong and the parents came to see me after considering more unconventional methods. Again, the parents refused to allow me to help that child. Why? For the same reason. Their whole life they believed in only what science could support, in what their doctors said, and in traditional medicine. Some people would rather put their own children in danger than consider alternatives outside of their belief system. Even when they know that doctors have been unsuccessful for years in determining the illness or in stopping the suffering, they cannot try something that could potentially help their child. These are the situations that I find difficult to face.

6

IS WHAT I DO ACCEPTED IN SOCIETY?

That answer varies and for many reasons. It varies due to country, region, nationality, and religion. It varies due to a person's gender, age and education, as well as upbringing.

In North America, we are a relatively new society and our countries are very young compared to European countries and especially places like the Middle East, China and India. The one exception is the natives of North America. In the Americas, natives have known about the spirit world for a long time.

In some countries like Mexico and India and Nepal, the spirit world is discussed openly in society and at the dinner table. It is not taboo. People in such countries who do not believe in the spirit realm, or angels and demons, are the exception and not the rule.

In North America, it is the opposite, but that is slowly changing due to the popularity of meditation and the renewed interest in spirituality. The influx of immigrants from all over the world has also helped spread word of the supernatural and the spirit world. People like me are now more openly talked about albeit not as openly as in other societies and countries.

Younger people are beginning to discover the whole spiritual concept. It's slowly being accepted, yet many of us are still skeptical. It is often women who are more interested in the spirit world, as women are often more open-minded than men. This is a general observation, and there are obviously exceptions. Because this is a relatively new way of thinking in North America, people often get confused and tricked and fall for the charlatans, fakes and phonies. People from certain cultures have more experience when it comes to spiritual matters, and a fake can be spotted a mile away.

I take it as a personal compliment that so many of my clients are immigrants. Even more of a blessing and compliment is the fact that I have clients and followers in many other countries outside Canada and the U.S.

7
BEING HEAVEN'S MESSENGER COMES WITH GREAT SACRIFICE

I often get calls, messages and texts from people telling me how cool it is to do what I do and how they would absolutely love to have my job! And I always respond, "No you wouldn't." Having these abilities is a huge blessing, and I wouldn't change it for anything in the world because I get to help people. I know it's my purpose in life and I couldn't be more blessed. Furthermore, I get to work for heaven, and there's nothing better. I couldn't ask for a better boss in the universe, and no better boss exists than the one that I work for.

But my gift comes with tremendous sacrifice and 99.99 percent of people would run away at the thought of the sacrifice that they would have to make.

Those who think it would be cool to fight evil spirits and demons would be terrified were they to come face to face with a real demon or have someone possessed look at them and say the things they say and do the things they do. Very few would have the courage and conviction to stand their ground with demons and go into battle like I do.

And this sacrifice doesn't just affect me; it affects my entire family. First of all, Maya and I are extremely connected, energetically and soul-wise, going back over many, many lifetimes, so very often, she can feel what I call an echo of what I feel. When I'm working on somebody energetically, she will feel a little buzzing, or energy, a vibration, or pulse, in her head. Also, because I work so much, day and night, trying to help as many people as I can, it puts a burden of responsibility on her to look after our five kids, all of whom have a special gift and therefore require special attention. She gives up all of her time and focuses all of her energy on what the family needs. This is a huge sacrifice, one she lovingly makes. Nor am I around as often as she or our children would like.

Furthermore, being so connected to me, and because evil wouldn't dare try to attack me, very often evil will go after her. It's a sacrifice she has to deal with almost every single day, with entities harassing her. All of my children have to face the same issue with entities harassing them, and very often, going after them while they sleep. (When we sleep, we open the door to the spirit world. Entities can often attack us and even harm us physically via the dream world.).

As can be imagined by anyone who understands energy (everything in the universe is energy), having this gift means that an incredible amount of energy from heaven comes into my body. The human body is not made to handle this amount of energy. In the same way that light bulbs and electrical appliances can handle only a maximum amount of energy (otherwise the light bulb can explode or the appliance can short-circuit), doing what I do surpasses the maximum capacity exponentially. With heavenly energy flowing through my body 24 hours a day, every day, I am exhausted and burned out, emotionally and physically.

On an even deeper sacrifice, one that I openly choose to make, I suffer the stigmata (defined by the Catholic Church as the marks or the pain of the crucifixion Jesus suffered). I suffer what Jesus suffered on the Cross, to a much lesser extent, of course. What we see in movies and on the internet, and read in books about stigmata is usually completely false. Countries with big Catholic populations are those who are most familiar with stigmata, like Italy, Spain, Portugal, Brazil, and Mexico, among others.

Stigmata is something very few people suffer from, throughout history in fact. I suffer the pain and also have the marks manifest themselves occasionally before quickly vanishing. I suffer from pain in the hands and feet 24 hours a day, There is no end to the pain, but I am used to it so the pain is bearable. I also get pains in my back that can last for minutes, and sometimes hours when it's at its worst. Suffering the stigmata every single day puts me in a position where I can work very closely with heaven. The point of my suffering a little of what Jesus suffered allows me to connect with Him even more, on a much deeper level. Suffice it to say that the holes in my hands created by the nails being driven into them are where the light shoots out from. I fight demons and sickness by becoming a vessel for heavenly light that enters me and comes out of my hands. Stigmata is not necessarily bloody. For those who suffer the stigmata, it manifests in marks, and for others, it's just pain that is felt. In my case, it's both. The marks come and go quickly. The pain, however, lasts 24 hours a day and ranges in intensity. So aside from the fact that my body's already completely burned out, I have tremendous pain 24 hours a day in my hands and in my feet, and very often in my back. People have witnessed me falling to the floor, screaming in pain due to where Jesus got the spear while He was on the Cross. People suffering the stigmata experience it from time to time and it lasts seconds or minutes at most. It is not 24/7 pain like mine. The truth is that very few people have ever actually legitimately gotten it. Highly spiritual people can often see round holes in my hands and some have seen the light in the palm of my hands where the nails went in. Some of my clients have even witnessed light shooting out of my hands.

I'm going to take sacrifice one step further. We all know that, throughout history, anyone who has ever made a difference, a real difference in the world, anyone who has spread the light, goodness and kindness, anyone who has combatted evil or the shadow, has at some point made much sacrifice. Nothing great can be accomplished without sacrifice.

Something that weighs heavily on my psyche is the fact that I can't help everyone, like I want to be able to. When I'm not allowed to help someone by heaven, for whatever reason, it hurts me. It hurts my soul. Why would I not be allowed to help someone with pain, sickness or disease? Sometimes, we are meant to go through these situations. We all have certain challenges in life to help us grow and often they can be physical challenges. Sometimes our pain and sickness are karma because of past life experiences or even things we did in this life.

One time I was contacted by someone regarding their parent who was sick with a variety of issues and was experiencing a lot of pain. Under normal circumstances, I would have been able to help this individual by easing some of the pain or health issues. But this time, I was told I could not help. Heaven made this clear to me, that the parent absolutely had to experience all of his physical ailments, and I had to tell my client that I couldn't help her parent. Sometimes I can help, but not fully. I can help alleviate the situation but not help completely. It all comes down to what I am allowed or not allowed to do.

Another situation that weighs heavily on me is when someone calls me or comes to see me in sickness, and I know that I can help them and save their life, for example. But when I explain that through God's heavenly light, I can help them, they tell me that they don't believe in this and they refuse to give me permission to help them. Sometimes a parent brings me a child who is dying, or is possessed. I need permission from the parent to help that child, and they don't give me permission to do so because they don't believe I can save that child, and they can't open their mind to that possibility. Certainly it isn't my fault that I cannot help that person or that child, but it still weighs on me knowing that I could have saved them.

When I tell somebody, "Look, I can help your child who is dying. I just need permission. Let's get started," and they refuse, after which the child dies, I have to live with the knowledge that had they only given me permission, I could have saved that child's life. This is a very heavy burden to carry.

So, there's physical, spiritual, and emotional sacrifice. Speaking of emotional sacrifice - and this is a deep and personal subject for me - were I to open up my emotions completely, I would not be able to do my work because I see terrible things on a daily basis. I see so much pain and suffering. Even helping so many people, and feeling the intense joy of doing so, would be overwhelming for me, so I turn off my emotional tap, so to speak. I become a little bit like a rock to be able to do what I need to do.

Imagine someone coming to see me because their child committed suicide, and I can see and feel the parents' pain, and then see the joy they feel when I contact that child's spirit and I'm speaking to the child in heaven. Watching the parent go through that emotion would be enough to completely destroy me, doing this day in and day out. Opening my emotional tap would wear me down, so I keep it closed. Unfortunately, when this tap is closed, it's closed for everyone, including my family, which means that perhaps I don't show the type of emotion that I should and would love to, for Maya and our children.

Maya also suffers the stigmata; not at the same level as me, but she suffers incredibly intense pain too. Our kids have to witness this as well, which is hard for them.

And finally, I don't get very much sleep, because it's very hard to turn off that "switch" that connects me to the spirit world.

For all these reasons, when people tell me that it's wonderful to have this gift, I tend to wonder if they'd change their mind knowing the sacrifices that this job requires.

I've had hundreds of people ask me to train them. Over the years, I've only chosen four people whom I felt had a legitimate gift. These four people were born with a gift that came from the light, and they wanted to do good with it. Only one person finished my course. The others all dropped out when they understood the real and true sacrifice that needed to be made.

Furthermore, not everyone understands or believes, or is open to what I do; some people even despise me for it. I've lost contact with friends and family members because they are not open-minded enough to want to understand what I do, so there is that sacrifice as well.

Let me be very clear: to work in the light, to make a difference in this world, everyone must be ready to make their own personal sacrifice in whatever manifestation that sacrifice takes.

8

HAUNTED HOMES AND EXORCISMS

There are many people today claiming to be mediums, gurus, intuitives, healers, sensitives, spiritual teachers, psychics, shamans - in fact worldwide, there is a very small fraction of them who can actually do what they claim. That number decreases further when it comes to clearing haunted homes and performing exorcisms. It's interesting to note that most so-called haunted house specialists will always do one of two things: they will enter a home, throw some holy water and burn some sage, maybe chant a little bit, spew some verses from the bible, and then claim that the house is no longer haunted, or they come in with fancy machines that detect energy. Anyone can do either of those things, but they cannot effectively destroy demons or free ghosts caught between the physical and spiritual realms.

Anyone can walk in off the street with a fancy camera, light or other tool that detects energy (and of course, entities, whether it be a ghost, an angel, demon or spirit, are simply a form of energy, in the same way the entire universe is energy). Then what happens? They confirm that there is/are entities and leave, doing absolutely nothing about it. That doesn't help the family with the haunted home whatsoever. Neither does burning some sage and throwing holy water. Holy water is nice, and sage smells nice, but these do nothing to get rid of entities. Ghosts must be crossed over to the other side. Demons must be destroyed.

A ghost is a soul that is stuck in the physical environment, which makes it different from a spirit, which has already crossed into the spirit world. Very few people can clear a haunted home, and those who have witnessed me do so, see that I go in simply using my hands. I see things with my eyes, and I get rid of them just with my hands, as heaven sends light through my hands to do so.

Haunted homes are no joke. It might sound like fun and games, and the stuff of fiction, but it's a very real and potentially disturbing and destructive environment. Even so, people generally wait until the situation is dire before contacting me for help. It's easy enough to understand: those sharing their space with a ghost or evil spirit usually don't want to believe that this is the case. It's as if they insist it's the last thing it could possibly be. They want to believe that they were simply tired, or they were stressed, or they didn't see correctly, when they witness something unexplainable happen in their home.

I warn people not to wait, that it can escalate at any moment. I've had cases where people were in danger and they still chose to do nothing about it because they simply refused to be open-minded enough to believe that there were entities in their home causing havoc and wishing them harm.

Possession is an even deeper, powerful topic of discussion. You can find a spiritual leader, whether it be a priest, rabbi or guru, who all claim to perform exorcisms. I can assure you that you can count the people who actually can, on two hands. This is why I get contacted from all over the world, specifically for haunted homes and for exorcisms, because so few people have this type of expertise. And again, nowadays, you can find so-called exorcists in almost every city, yet most of them cannot do what they claim that they can do, and they charge exorbitant rates as well.

People need to understand that possession is very real, and it is dangerous. I tell people that there is never a happy ending when it comes to a demonic possession. The person who is possessed will either lose their mind and end up in a mental institution, or very often, they will commit suicide or harm someone else, landing them in jail. There is no happy ending. The demon won't simply leave the body and take off and say "thanks for the ride - I'm outta here. Take your body back." Once a demon gets a body, it wants to keep it.

I've heard mind-boggling things that so-called exorcists claim to do, and there is a reason that these people - and that includes those in the Vatican - are never successful. In documented cases seen on

Youtube or in movie documentaries and in books, (whether it be the Vatican or other religious organization, or individuals claiming to be exorcists), most of the time, the person they try to help dies. There are movies that have come out about it, documentaries, books about famous exorcist cases – these possessed people all die. In my case, not only do I have an astounding success rate, not only has nobody ever died, no one has even gotten hurt. Nobody who has ever come to see me, who is possessed, has ever gotten hurt, and that includes parents who have brought me young children who were possessed.

I've seen everything you can possibly imagine. I've fought all forms of demons; different strengths and types, and I haven't failed, because heaven uses my hands to fight the shadow. I fight the shadow with light. Light always defeats the shadow.

Even for fakes, very few will claim to be exorcists or haunted house specialists. Only the very confident or adventurous fakes will do so. Most simply claim to be mediums, psychics, energy workers, or healers of some sort. These people who claim to be exorcists or haunted home specialists think it's cool, but it's not so cool to come face to face with entities and demons. It's cool to destroy them, because the light always wins and the shadow always loses. Evil gets kicked to the curb. But it is not fun and games to fight demons on a one-on-one level. Very few people in the world can do so. Even fewer can do so successfully.

I'm often asked if what we see on TV or in movies is accurate with regards to haunted homes and exorcisms. Much of it is not. Obviously a TV show or movie will be embellished to make it seem more scary, to have more action, but some of it is indeed accurate. Things do move around the house, people do see shadows. People do get attacked by entities, and I've been called to homes where people were thrown down the stairs. I've been called to homes where 500 lb. objects were floating around. I've been contacted by people whose baby was being moved in the crib by entities. Mothers whose 4-, 5-, or 6-year-old children were able to pick up one of the parents with one hand and throw them across the room. I've seen these children who are speaking Latin or other foreign languages in deep voices, with eyes completely black. I've seen these children, and I've helped them.

I've witnessed the most severe cases. I've been to a home where a child was hanging from a chandelier, while holding a loaded gun. I've helped people who were spewing things out of their mouths and choking and coughing uncontrollably.

If I were asked to describe the craziest home I've cleansed or exorcism I've performed, it would be very difficult to answer. Each case is unique, disturbing and powerful in its own right. Many of them, to the normal human mind, would be considered insane. It's no walk in the park to do this, and it's something most people would not want to witness.

JARRED NEIL

I urge people, if you think your home is haunted, if you think someone you know is possessed, please don't wait. At some point, the situation will escalate and get much worse.

9

BEWARE THE WOLF IN SHEEP'S CLOTHING

This chapter will no doubt upset many people in the spiritual field. Some of you may already be current friends or acquaintances. When I have discussed this in the past, many people did not want to hear this, did not like to hear this. However, truth is truth. Light is light. It must be said. When you are chosen by heaven, you are chosen to be born with a gift. The same way one cannot learn to play basketball like Michael Jordan, or sing like Elvis Presley or Michael Jackson, or play hockey like Bobby Orr or Wayne Gretzky, one cannot learn to do what I do. One must be born with it. It is a natural gift, an innate ability, and although many people like the idea of being able to wake up one day and decide that they'd like to be a medium or a psychic, a shaman or an exorcist, they cannot.

You can certainly take courses and become better at something than you were before, but you cannot learn the actual talent or ability itself. It must be there from the get-go. Anyone working in the light, as I am, is born with it. Sure, we need to understand it and develop it, the same way that singers, actors and sports heroes do. You cannot learn to be at such a level; you must be born with it. And this upsets a lot of people, because many people take courses to learn how to speak to the angels or the deceased, or they read a book on how to do tarot card reading and think this is actually, legitimately, from heaven. People can take a weekend seminar or month-long course to learn to be a shaman, or be taught to heal. Well, I have news for you: You cannot. It comes from heaven. This is a fact. You are either born with it, or you are not. So, do all these people taking courses to become a shaman have a legitimate gift? For many of them, absolutely not. Let's get real here: some shamans have studied for 30 years in the jungle to get to the level that they are at, even though they were born with some ability to heal others. If you work in the light, you need to be born with it and of course, some people are.

There are different levels of spiritual gift. My wife Maya is a perfect example. Some people with a legitimate gift in the light can do similar things. Some can speak to the deceased. Some can get visions. Some can interpret dreams. Some can help those who are sick. There are certainly people with a real spiritual gift in some way, shape or form, albeit at a very minimal level. Not everyone is meant to do what I do and especially not with the same ability as I have.

I never took a course on how to speak to the angels, or to the deceased, or how to use my hands to help someone with sickness, disease, or who is in tremendous pain. I never took a course on how to walk into a haunted home and get rid of entities, or how to kill demons who have possessed a body. I was born with this gift; I was born to be a vessel for heaven. I simply learned what that gift entailed, and developed it to ensure I was using this gift to the best of my abilities, so that I could help as many people as possible.

Some people who take courses do get some type of ability, but it's not coming from above, it's coming from below. It's not coming from the light, it's coming from the shadow. And this is why all these people taking courses are going to be upset: People learning to play with energy, such as reiki, or how to heal, I have news for you and you probably already know it. You're not working with angels; you're working with demons. You're not working with heaven; you're working with hell. You are not working with the light, you are working with the shadow, and I know this. Many of you know it too, and you do it anyway. And I'm not sure what's worse, those who know it and do it anyway, or the fact that many aren't even aware of where they're getting their power source from or where this ability comes from. The shadow is always waiting for somebody to wake up one day and say, "Hey, it would be cool to talk to angels, or to talk with the deceased, to heal someone who is dying." Shadow is always waiting to help someone in such a situation. And the courses that are given are created by the shadow. There are many good people who take these courses, who have all the right intentions to help others, yet they don't realize where their power source is coming from. Client confidentiality is of the utmost importance to me, so I won't name names, but many so-called reiki masters have sat in my office because they were possessed. Many so-called energy workers have reached out to me for help when they understood that evil had taken over them and they needed help, and they had no legitimate gift to get rid of it. Many so-called mediums and psychics, clairvoyants - call them what you like - many of the people working in my field (even though I don't consider what I do as a 'field', it is what I do, it is who I am), have come to me behind closed doors, behind the scenes, seeking real help because they understood that a) they can't do what they claim they can do, and b) they understood where their source was coming from and they needed a higher source, one in the light, to help them combat it. And as I've stated, I'll never mention names, but many who advertise claiming to do what I do have come to see me for help. They claimed to help others, but they needed help themselves, and this is extremely dangerous in my opinion.

The same way a person is chosen from above to be a painter, an artist, singer or dancer, athlete or motivational speaker, regardless of the field of choice or expertise, each person has a chosen path on earth, and so it is in the spiritual field.

All the fake gurus, intuitives, spiritual advisors, and all the other fancy names that they choose to come up with: Let it be known that the Creator is watching, the universe is watching, and karma is

HEAVEN'S MESSENGER

very, very real. I will let the Creator, the universe and karma deal with those of you who are fakes and frauds, those who work in the shadow.

10

FAKES, FRAUDS AND CON ARTISTS

In every field, you can find fakes, frauds, and con artists, and the spiritual industry is no exception. Charlatans, phonies, scammers, whatever you want to call them, are everywhere. This is particularly disheartening because they prey on people who are vulnerable, who are looking for hope, who may be desperate, who are willing to believe absolutely anything.

The most sought-after spiritual service offered is clairvoyance. Because this is such a popular service, fakes claiming to have clairvoyant or psychic abilities are on every street corner. Psychic hotlines are a multi-million dollar business, and all the people working these hotlines are frauds. These so-called psychics will tell people exactly what they want to hear, and gullible people will believe them. Anyone with a God-given ability to predict events is not working a hotline.

Any fortune teller is a scam artist or is working for the shadow. Life is not Disney World. Life is not perfect. Not everything is going to be good. So anyone who only tells you good things, like a fortune teller does (because they only talk about money, fame, fortune and happiness) are not working in the light. Card readers also fall into this category because many provide only positive information and besides, anyone with a legitimate gift does not need cards; they would receive direct messages. Furthermore, anything that anyone can learn or that is easy to learn is not legitimate.

Now let's talk about mediums and psychics. Because of their popularity through television, they are in big demand. And because of this demand, so many fakes and frauds can be found. They give general information that can apply to anyone. Everyone wants to believe that the spirit world exists; people want to believe their loved ones are still around, and we would all love to speak with our loved ones again. It's easy for a medium to sit with you and tell you that your loved one who has passed loves you, and isn't suffering anymore. Heaven is beautiful; there is no suffering, there is nothing bad, only good. Your loved one is in a beautiful place and they love you. Anyone off the street can tell you that.

Another sign of a fake is when a medium or psychic asks for information up front. Birth date, job, marital status, name and relationship of the person you want to contact, etc. Generally, in a good session with a medium, they can tell you one or more things about your loved one that they could not possibly have known. When someone comes to see me to contact a deceased loved one, I don't need any information, other than a first name, and only when the client is in front of me, never before a session.

It does happen on very rare occasions that I cannot

communicate with a deceased loved one. It's the same as when we can't reach a loved one who is alive; spirits are also unavailable sometimes. When that happens, I let my clients know and they don't pay. It's that simple. This happens less than five percent of the time.

Another sure sign of a fake is when a medium or psychic starts giving you dates and specifics of when something is going to happen, or the exact time when something is going to happen. This is clearly fraud, since the spirit world doesn't work like that. There is no concept of time in the spirit world. Past, present and future all happen simultaneously. It is only in the physical world that we follow a linear time frame.

When you walk into a medium or psychic's office and you get a negative feeling, or the hair on your arm stands up, trust your intuition and get out. Also (and this may come as a surprise, since many well-known mediums or psychics do this), those who work in front of a large audience are also frauds. It's very easy to stand up in front of an audience and say, "There's a spirit here, and this spirit is holding his heart...Is there anyone who had a brother, an uncle, father, boyfriend, or cousin who died of a heart attack?" Well, guess what, half the audience will raise their hand.

Another clear indication of a fake is when these so-called mediums and psychics talk about their spirit guides, and how these spirit guides provide them with information. I know the names of the angels with whom I speak, and I know what they look like. 99% of the time, these so-called mediums will not know the names of whoever it is they are talking to in the spirit world, and can't describe them either. Or the medium/psychic might say it's her aunt Mary who is giving her messages. It's not the job of spirits or souls who have passed on to sit there and pass along messages! Or when someone says they have a gift that's been passed down from generation to generation, and they don't mention heaven, or angels - it's they who have the gift and it's not coming from heaven or God, and they're "special." This is a sure sign that you're dealing with a fake or that this person is working for the shadow.

Something I hear often from those claiming to have a gift similar to mine or claiming to do what I do is this: "I choose to keep my gift a secret," or "I choose not to use my gift," or "I work quietly behind the scenes and nobody knows." Does this make them phonies? Liars? Cowards if they do have a gift and don't use it? On several occasions I have asked those claiming to have the same gift as I do, why I don't know them, or why I have never heard of them. It just doesn't feel right when the answer I get is that they choose not to use their gift or they use it quietly and stay out of the spotlight. Can this be possible? I suppose so. Would it be right, make sense or be cowardly? I will let you decide the answer.

Now, let's discuss fees. If someone says it will cost $1000 to contact your mother who has passed, don't give in. We all need to charge a fee to make a living, but it shouldn't cost an enormous amount. If someone says it will cost $15,000, $20,000 or even only $5,000 to get the demon out of your child, run far away. There is a difference between someone making a living and someone being greedy.

As I mentioned earlier, people who seek out mediums or psychics are in need of guidance, and in some cases, are desperate to communicate with the spirit of a deceased loved one. Parents who have a child who is possessed are desperate to have their precious child back. Anyone working in the light will not rob you blind.

Also, anyone claiming to be a guru, a leader, someone that you should look up to, someone that you should follow and worship – is a fake and is working in the shadow. They are absolutely not working for heaven. Guaranteed. Also beware of someone who tries to push many services on you; for instance, they see an evil entity attached to you and for a fee, will remove it, when you only need another service. If you're looking on social media for someone, beware of any type of fancy term, like spiritual advisor or spiritual counselor. These people probably can't do what they claim they can do, and they most likely charge big fees. Don't waste your money.

Another service that's becoming trendy is past life regression. I refuse to be involved in this for a few reasons. For starters, how will knowing who you were in the past change your life now? It won't. It's useless information. Furthermore, it can be dangerous. Those who offer this service will argue this, since it's how they make money, but bringing someone's mind back to a past life is dangerous as they could potentially get stuck there! Imagine thinking you are a little girl in Russia in 1800 while living in New York City in 2018. Don't fall for the scam of those so-called mediums and psychics who tell you they need to "cut the cord" or ties from your past life holding you back...it's nonsense!

I am not a fan of any spiritual group activity, especially not group meditations. Furthermore, any so-called medium or psychic who performs group services is a charlatan and fake and I will explain why:

GROUP MEDITATION

I don't recommend group meditation at all. When done properly, meditation puts one in a sleep-like state, and this opens a door to the spirit world which is how spirits can talk to regular people. Demons can harass and even attack people in this state. Also, when that door is open, nobody can control what comes through it, let alone stop it. Very few worldwide can tell the difference between good and bad and that includes so-called gurus and meditation experts, mediums and psychics.

Evil does not always show itself. The devil appears with a smile and roses and a rainbow, not with horns and a pitchfork, and many meditations end in someone getting possessed.

Now imagine a group meditation. The bigger the group, the bigger the door to the spirit world that gets opened, meaning much more can come through that door. Now understand very few so-called gurus or meditation teachers or experts have any real ability or knowledge and cannot look after themselves in a meditation or detect what is good or evil. How can they then do so for a large group of people? They cannot! They are supposed to be responsible for all those in the meditation group, but have no ability to help or protect them.

GROUP READINGS

Group sessions are complete nonsense. I'll give you a few reasons why that is. Any real and true gift or ability in the light comes from heaven, from the light. Just to interpret messages and feelings for one person can be difficult. How can someone do so for many at the same time? It's impossible. Furthermore, every person has an energy and aura field. That means every additional person brings more energy. How can someone possibly properly understand messages with so much energy around? Also, how can they know for whom the message is for? They cannot! Doing group readings is a very dishonest way to make a living.

It is too easy to fool the general public with generic or vague messages which people can determine might have meaning for them, which is why most so-called mediums or psychics will give very vague information or outright lie with specific things for the future. Another all-too-common tactic with very popular so-called mediums and psychics is having people working for them in the crowd, taking notes and passing along information via ear pieces.

GROUP CONTACT OF DECEASED

For most of the same reasons mentioned in group reading, contact of deceased mega group sessions are fraudulent and bogus. The fakes use the same tricks and tools to fool the masses as they do in group readings. People actually pay each time to go to a group reading simply hoping their deceased loved one will come through. Firstly, spirits don't just hang around waiting for someone to contact them. Spirits can and have come to me without my calling on them, however it is rare. Usually I call on them to come to me. This nonsense of people claiming spirits come to them all the time is the oldest scam trick in the book. Furthermore, how would they know who the spirit was and for whom it was coming for? With hundreds of people in the audience, how would the so-called medium know? I most often call a specific spirit using a picture or object they owned and was important to them. (The reason for this is that there's a residue of their energy attached to the object or picture.). Notice how the medium on stage rarely gives specific information? It's usually very generic such as, "They love you and miss you." Really? Good to know! It's pure hogwash! If there are 500 audience members and the medium asks, "Who here had a brother or father or son or uncle or male figure who had a heart attack? There is a spirit here holding their heart."

Chances are most of the audience would raise their hand!

I have been offered big money to do both group readings and group contact of the deceased sessions and I refuse every time. It is dishonest and cannot be done.

Beware of so-called card readers and those claiming to have a message for all people, for all of humanity. Each of us is unique and different. How can someone claim that each of us is meant to receive the exact same message at that moment in time? It's pure nonsense. Same with someone who pulls a card claiming they have a message for all of humanity. First of all, anyone can learn to pull cards which are nonsense and meant for entertainment purposes only. That being said, look at this scenario. Person A picks a card in New York at noon EST and claims archangel Raphael has a message for every human. OK. What about Person B who picked a card in London which is four hours ahead and claims their card for humanity was from Gabriel and it was a completely different message. Now Person C will pick a card at 11 a.m. Pacific time which is 3 hours behind New York, and claim the card is from archangel Michael and it has a different meaning for all humans. See the nonsense here?

11

THE NEW AGE MOVEMENT

"The road to hell is paved with good intentions." This proverb was written long before the New Age movement spread through Western countries in the 1970s and 1980s, but it certainly holds true here. Tarot reading, astrology, yoga, meditation techniques, channeling and the use of crystals were integrated into the movement to assist personal transformation. Many of these spiritual disciplines are gaining in popularity in North America.

I refer to the New Age movement as the hocus-pocus, nonsense movement and it is not energy from the light, it is from the shadow. I am 100% sure of this. As I've mentioned, to be chosen by the light, you are born with it. The Creator wants you to work on behalf of heaven, and it is simply not something you pick up one day. The New Age movement is filled with all kinds of silly things that people can simply take a course on. Let's take card reading, reiki, and other energy treatments for example. What are my feelings and thoughts on such things? They come from the shadow. They come from the devil. First of all, someone with a real gift does not need a tool. Someone who claims to be able to go into a haunted home and find entities should not need an infrared camera or any type of device that detects energy.

When I go into a home, I use only my eyes and my hands. Someone with a real gift shouldn't need cards. The angels speak to me directly as do the deceased. I don't need cards. Anyone who needs a tool to accomplish this either doesn't have a real gift, or is getting their energy from the shadow.

On paper, the New Age movement looks so wonderful. It's all about love and peace, and bettering oneself. But how many movements throughout history looked good on paper? Communism looked good on paper, even though over the last 100 years, upwards of 150 million people were killed (and that's just these countries' own people). Communist dictators are murdering their own people; never mind the wars or other side effects of communism.

Another example would be the concept that evil doesn't exist. This is one of the lies the devil wants us to believe, that he doesn't exist. Because if you don't believe that evil exists, you don't have to fight against it. You don't have to stand for the light against the shadow. But evil certainly does exist. So, for all the people subscribing to the particular New Age movement theory that there is no evil, or that evil is one with the light, chooses not to fight evil, chooses to accept it.

Another concept in the New Age movement is that evil does exist, but you don't need to fight it. All you need is love; give it a hug and tell it how beautiful it is. Never mind that archangel Mikha'el fought the devil with a sword of light, and that sometimes, love is not enough. Some people don't feel that they need to battle evil. Like, if only somebody had given Hitler a hug, man, things would have been different. Millions wouldn't have died. If only someone had given a hug to Osama Bin Laden, things would have been different. Or if Stalin had only been given a bouquet of roses, millions of people might not have perished. Or Charles Manson, all he needed was a pat on the back and to be told how nice his beard was. Nonsense! That's what I think about the New Age movement.

That's also what I think about group meditations, which is also an aspect of the New Age movement. This whole idea of having hundreds or thousands of people doing a group meditation at the same time with a fake so-called guru who claims to be leading the group in a meditation; well, that same so-called guru - who can't even protect himself in a meditation - how is he going to protect a group of dozens, hundreds or thousands of people from whatever comes through that door? When meditation is done properly, you're putting yourself in a sleep-like state and you're opening the door to the spirit world, and you have no control over which spirits come through that door, good or evil.

So, suffice it to say that I'm not a fan of the crystal ball, or cards, because they're tools. Furthermore, as I've said, you need to be born with this gift if you're working for the light, and anyone can purchase a deck of cards and take a course on how to read them. Courses are now being offered on how to speak to the deceased or to angels and anyone off the street can take them. Reiki, which originated in Japan as energy work, is taught in North America now, and every Tom, Dick, Harry and Sally can take the course and within a week, become a certified reiki practitioner. Then, within a short amount of time, he or she can become a reiki master. These people are playing around with energy, and a lot of them have no idea that this energy is coming from the shadow, not the light. It's all complete nonsense. It's all from the devil, from the shadow.

The New Age movement has very dangerous practices; most, if not all of them, coming from the shadow.

12

SPIRIT STREET SMARTS

Here I explain the entities I connect with in the spirit realm, as well as my thoughts on reincarnation at the end of this chapter.

First of all, everything in the universe is made of energy. Angels, demons, spirits and ghosts are no exception.

Spirits can be good or bad. They are people who died and crossed over to the spirit world. Good ones obey the laws of the universe and remain in what we call heaven, or the light. They can and sometimes manifest themselves in the physical world to let us know they are around and they also visit us in our dreams, because it's easier for them.

Any spirits hanging around in the physical realm are not good, contrary to popular belief. (Good spirits have so much more to learn, and aren't supposed to be hanging around the physical world.). Bad spirits can and will harm. They break the natural laws and will hang around the physical realm. They will work with demons although there are many more demons than bad spirits. Bad spirits are those who died and refuse to go to the light and prefer the shadow or what people think of as hell. Also contrary to popular belief, hell is not down below and heaven is not above per se. They are all around us, as spirit and physical realms are side by side.

Demons are from hell, so to speak, but are not spirits who are so bad they become demons. Demons can be physical or spiritual, meaning they can dwell in the physical realm as demons in actual human form and they walk and live among us as such. They can dwell in spiritual realm which is the most common, although they can and will possess human bodies and/or attach themselves to humans. Perhaps surprisingly, the most common form of entity in a haunted location is a demon; very few people worldwide have the ability to destroy them.

Ghosts are souls that are stuck in the physical world. Again, contrary to silly opinions, they are not being punished. They are not bad, however, a ghost can be bad if the person themselves was bad. Ghosts are mostly good; it's just that their spirit or soul never crossed over to the spirit realm. In essence, the spirit is caught in a physical world with no physical attributes. Ghosts are actually suffering. Most times when a human sees or hears an entity, it is a ghost, as ghosts are forced to have some physicality to them. Often a ghost is seen or heard at the same time or same place where they got stuck.

A ghost often chooses to stay behind for two main reasons: Either they don't know they are dead, or they thought they would be closer to their family or loved ones, which is a false belief. They are not closer. Ghosts can be crossed over to the spirit realm, but not on their own. Very few people can do this. I am one of the few. It's important to note that most so-called experts in this field have no actual knowledge or real experience dealing with entities as I do. It's the same for most so-called ghost hunters who have no ability whatsoever, and rely solely on fancy machines that detect energy, noise, etc. They may be able to detect a ghost, but they are not able to cross it over to the spirit realm.

How do spirits communicate with us? They don't speak the normal way since they have no mouth. They communicate to those who are open to it by image and feelings. They "show" us things. Very few people can communicate with them. Spirits also sometimes speak to regular people via dreams. Spirits will often come to us in dreams to communicate with us. Someone open, like me, can sometimes have "words" planted in our mind. We "hear" some words.

There is no so-called no-man's land or place in the spirit realm where a soul is stuck as punishment. All souls go through a cleansing in the spirit realm before becoming one with the source, or God, again. Contrary to belief once more, those who commit suicide or are gay do not go to such a place or to hell. They very much go to heaven.

Magical and mystical creatures like fairies and vampires, shape shifters, werewolves, and what's real: Many of the fairy tales we hear are actually quite true and real, or at least have some truth to them. Witches are real. There are good as well as bad witches and a wide variety of types of witches. They are in the physical realm although they can often connect with the spirit realm. Vampires are also quite real and exist in both the physical and spiritual worlds. They are different from those we read about or see on TV. These vampires do not live forever. They do not suck blood. They do, however, suck energy. They will drain you of your positive energy. Fairies are less common but real and also exist in both worlds, although it is more common to see them in the spirit realm. Werewolves are not real if we go by what we see in movies, however, shape shifters are very real and often take the form of wolves.

I work closely with eight archangels, and truth be told, there are many more angels and archangels than most realize or understand. Most so-called experts in the spiritual field have no clue how many angels there are, who the angels truly are, or even what they look like. When we think of angels, we visualize them with wings and bodies, but in fact, angels are beings of pure light. They are God's messengers. They work directly for the Lord and were created as His messengers, and part of their responsibility is to help humanity and help guide us. They manifest as having wings and bodies to make us more comfortable.

HEAVEN'S MESSENGER

The English word angel comes from the Greek word angelos which means messenger. Angels are not saints or well known people who became angels. They are pure light. They existed long before humanity ever did.

As I just mentioned, I work closely with eight archangels. Our relationship is similar to that of Jesus and I. Angels are always with me. They help me with clairvoyant visions and messages. They help me to clear haunted homes, help people who are sick and with disease and pain, and they of course help me with exorcisms. It is angelic light that comes into my body. The angels send me the light I use to fight disease and demons. My body is a vessel for them.

I have a guardian angel as does every human. One angel can be a guardian for millions of people. My guardian angel has literally helped save my life several times. He appears a certain way to me just as the other angels take a certain shape and appearance even though they don't need to, and in fact, they don't have a body. They are energy. They are light and only appear in certain ways to make it easier for us to connect with them and make us feel comfortable. They also don't have wings. They don't need them. They can be anywhere they want and be in several places at the same time. They appear with wings for the same reasons that they appear with a body and/or face. Mikha'el happens to be the archangel I work closest with. Each can do many things even though they all have a specialty. They are my guides. They have personalities. Some make me laugh and we even joke around sometimes. They remind me of things. They are therefore like friends, like family. Although angels have no gender, being made of energy, and therefore are not male or female, they are either more masculine or more feminine, and one of the archangels with whom I deal is more feminine.

Reincarnation absolutely exists. Some people claim we can live up to 99,000 times, however, this is not true. The average soul will return anywhere from 25-40 times. I estimate that I have been here 26 or 27 times; I don't know the specifics of my past lives, with the exception of three or four important ones which led me to be who I am. I knew Jesus well when He was alive, as I was there with Him. We were very close and now once again we are working together. In the future, I will explain in further detail how Jesus and I knew each other 2,000 years ago.

Three of my children come from a very high place in heaven. In fact, I can give you an idea of who they were: my youngest, Gabriel Mikael chose his own name, because he was close to the archangels who carry those names, Michael and Gabriel. He knew them very well. Two of my other children come from the same place. My other two children were not from that realm, however, anyone picking up the Old Testament can read about them. Trying times require special and holy souls and beings to be here on earth to aid in the battle against evil, and it is for this reason that my children are here.

When déja vu happens, it is usually connected to a past life. When two people meet and feel like they know each other, but also know they never met before, these are souls meeting each other again from a previous life encounter. Some people think we can come back as an animal or rock as punishment. It's more complicated than that, because a part of our soul often comes back and not the whole soul. It's just a piece of the soul. I can speak to some spirits that have part of themselves here in human form. Powerful souls can have part of themselves in several people. So, can we come back as an animal or rock? I know that we can come back as an animal; I doubt very much we can come back as a rock. Our spirit is on a continual path of learning. It would be rather hard to grow spiritually as a rock!

13

CLAIRVOYANT SESSIONS

This is the most popular service I offer. The reason is simple: everyone is looking for hope. Everyone is searching for answers. Everyone wants to find the meaning in their life. We all want to know our destiny. People want to know why they are here and what they are meant to accomplish while here. They want to hear positive things so they have something to hope for and look forward to. It is basic human nature to want meaning in life and to want and hope for good things. Most people want to know what their future holds. This is why clairvoyance is the most common and sought-after spiritual service.

As a clairvoyant, I am able to see and predict things before they happen, and I've had countless amazing sessions with clients. One of the things I tell clients before a clairvoyant session is that I'm not a fortune teller. I will not tell them things that they want to hear; I will tell them what they need to hear. I am going to tell them what the angels show me, because I get my visions and messages from the angels above. Of course, it is my interpretation of what I'm seeing or hearing, but it's usually very accurate. Everything I see will be significant and potentially life-changing. As I've said before, I'm not in the business of guessing. Usually the visions I see are very clear to me, and if it's not clear to me, I let my clients know. These sessions can last an hour and a half, or they can last less than an hour. I never know how long a session could last, as I don't know what the angels will have to tell me. It's that simple.

Anything I see during a session is to help people, or to help avoid bad situations from happening. I've helped to predict and prevent terrible accidents from happening that would result in incredible injury or death, helped prevent sickness, and bad things happening to children. I've helped to prevent suicide, bad business decisions and bad relationship decisions. I've helped to prevent so many negative things from happening, but I've also been able to make many wonderful things happen, such as making proper relationship decisions, and positive decisions regarding work, health, vacation, and the purchase or selling of personal possessions.

I've seen names and faces of people who got involved in crimes, people who have committed murder; even how they dressed. I've seen how people were going to die or commit suicide if it wasn't prevented. I've seen a lot of sickness before it happened, and helped to prevent the sickness from occurring, with details of exactly where the sickness would occur and how it would occur if they didn't take certain steps. I've explained the steps to take to prevent sickness. I've seen exact intersections where an accident would happen, so that the accident could be avoided. Topics that are covered include finances, health, relationships, love, work and more.

Once in a while, I get a request from someone that I can't fulfill. One such time, a woman called me and began telling me that her husband left her and moved away. She mentioned that she didn't know where he went, but that she wanted him back and was willing to pay me whatever it took to find him, to play around in his head and to make him fall in love with her again. She was hoping that I could use some type of magic to convince him to fall back in love with her and come home. Needless to say, my answer to her was no, because first of all, I never go against anyone's free will, and two, even if I could figure out where he was, I would never, ever consider playing around in someone's head and make them do anything. She couldn't understand why I wouldn't do it. It was one of the weirdest requests I've had.

I've also had many requests to put curses on people, which is mind-blowing to me since I'm very clear with people that I work with angels, not demons! A curse always involves a demon; an angel is not going to put a curse on someone!

Sometimes people will ask me if they are cursed. I tell them that most people don't have the power to put a curse on someone. The person who wants to put a curse on someone would have to seek out someone who might have that ability. Perhaps someone dabbling in voodoo or black magic for the wrong reasons could do that, as they are dealing with demons. I've refused countless requests from people who had evil intentions and wanted me to use information for wrong reasons, or who wanted me to do something bad. Sometimes I can feel a bad energy coming from someone over the phone or even from an email, and I will tell them that I cannot help them and they will have to see someone else. I've been offered massive amounts of money to use my gift for the wrong reasons. I will never do anything that involves hurting others. In the same way that heaven won't allow me to go against someone's free will, I cannot use my gift for nefarious reasons or for profit only. This is also why working for heaven doesn't allow me to use my gift to win a lottery. If God wanted me to win the lottery, it would happen.

I'm very clear with potential clients that if they want to use my services for "fun," I will tell them to call someone else. I am not a circus show. The services I offer are very deep and real. If someone asks me if I read cards or if I'm a fortune teller, I let them know that I cannot help them!

I do not offer clairvoyant sessions over the phone, via email or Skype. The reason is simple: It's never as accurate as in person, and I want to offer the best service I can. This means that every session must be in person. I have helped sick people by distance when it was an emergency issue, and they could not come to me, however, it's a rare occurrence because it takes insane amounts of energy and time, and again, it doesn't work as well as in person.

Sometimes, the angels work in mysterious ways. I got a call one day from a woman who wanted to cancel her appointment that she had that evening. She had booked it three months previously and was really looking forward to it, she said, but she felt that something was preventing her from going. She kept emphasizing how she really wanted to see me, but felt that she should cancel for an unexplainable reason. Five minutes later, I received an email from a woman saying that it had been about six months since she wanted to book an appointment with me, but she kept putting it off. She said that just a few minutes prior to calling me, my name had popped into her head, and she instinctively knew (as if she had gotten a message from above) that she needed to see me. I told her that someone had just cancelled an appointment and asked if she could come that evening. She accepted, and as our session progressed, I saw an intersection where this lady would have an accident. I asked her if she had ever been to this specific intersection or if she would be going to this intersection, and she looked at me and said, "No, never." But then she said, "Oh my God, I actually have an appointment there tomorrow!" I said, "Please don't go, you will have a fatal car accident if you do."

You could say it was divine intervention when a woman cancelled her appointment for no apparent reason, leaving space for another woman to learn

HEAVEN'S MESSENGER

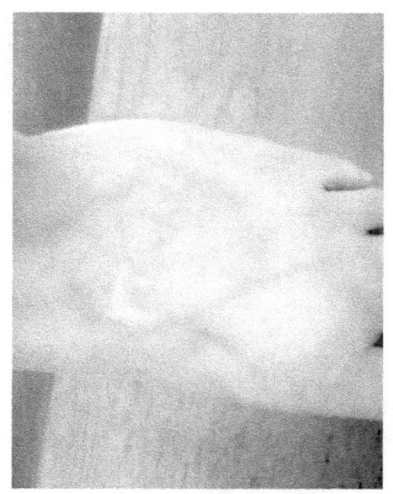

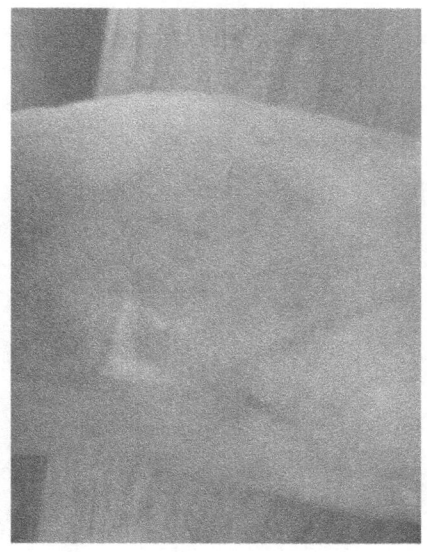

My foot after stigmata

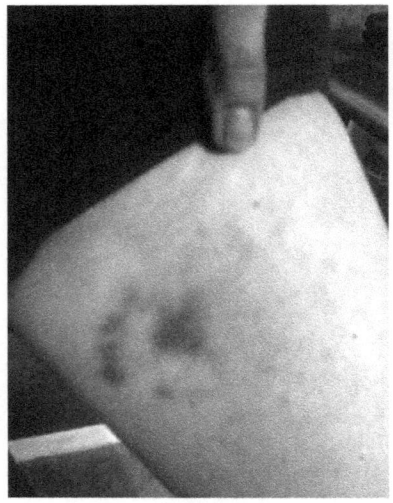

Paw or animal marks appearing on a client's leg that occurred while she slept.

Healing a dog with kidney failure. This dog did not have long to live, yet jumped off my table after our session and began running around my backyard.

HEAVEN'S MESSENGER

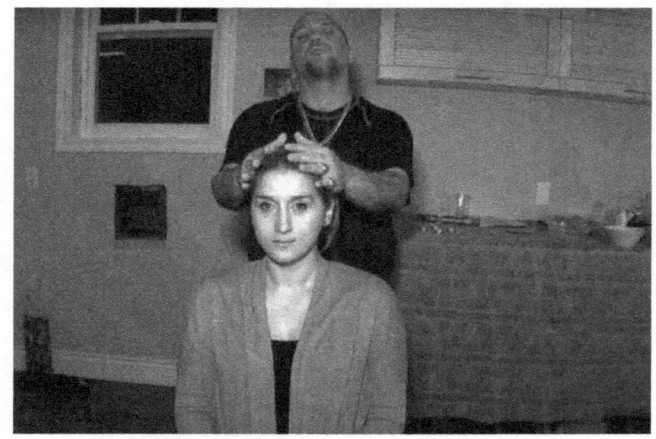

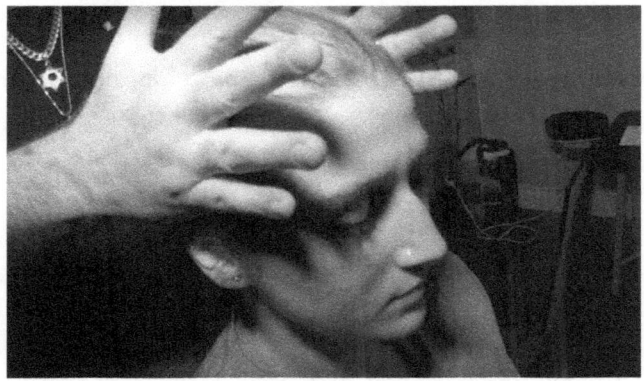

Finishing an exorcism on a client who was possessed after playing with a Ouija board.

Drawing that a possessed girl drew for me during an exorcism, (when the demon wasn't allowing her to speak).

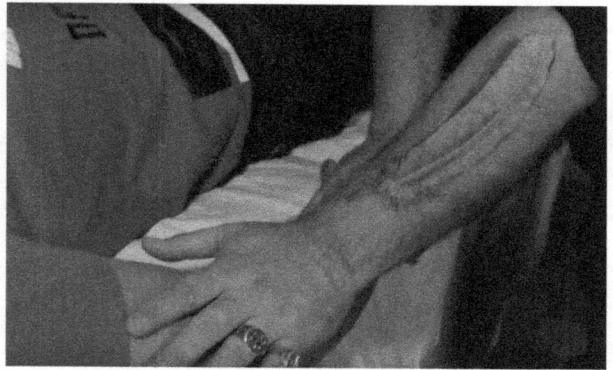

Performing a shamanic treatment for a man who was injured in a motorcycle accident.

The Beat 92.5 radio morning show crew and I at the Notman House in Montreal.

Image of a demon captured on camera at the Notman House.

My back tattoo of Archangel Michael

Screen capture of messages between Julia's friend and the demon inside Julia.

that she could avoid a fatal accident the very next day!

Another interesting session I can recall was of a woman who called me, speaking in a thick, European accent. She said to me, "I'm not sure I believe in this, but the other day, I was at a hotel attending a business event. It was a big event, and I decided to take a little break and go for a walk around the hotel grounds. At one point, I got tired and stopped to rest. I happened to look down at my feet, and between my feet was a business card, and it was yours. As I said, I have a hard time believing in this, but I didn't think it was a coincidence that of all the people who could find this business card on the ground, it was I. I believe that there's a message here and I need to see you as soon as possible." Of course, I agreed with her, because I know nothing happens by chance; nothing happens by coincidence.

We set up an appointment, and she came over. During our session, I was telling her what the first thing was that the angels were showing me (which often happens to be the most important thing), and this explained why she found my business card. I had seen her in an airplane with a man and a teenage girl. I saw the plane landing, and saw them getting picked up in a small car by another man. It was clear to me that this was in Europe somewhere, and shortly after they were picked up at the airport, they were involved in a car accident, where they all perished. So I looked at her and said, "Are you going to be taking a trip in the near future by plane, to

Europe?" And she looked at me in shock, and said, "Yes, in a couple of weeks. I'm actually moving back to Europe." I said, "Are you going with a man and a girl who appears to be in her teens?" "Yes, that's my husband and teenage daughter," she replied. I continued, "Are you being picked up by a male, as opposed to taking a cab, in a small car that looks like a Renaud or something similar?" And she said, "Oh my God, yes, that's our very good friend who is going to pick us up." I said to her, "Please change the date of your flight, because if you don't, you will all die in an accident. This is why the angels put that business card at your feet." We were both in shock at realizing that the angels wanted to save four lives: hers, her husband's, her daughter's and their friend's.

In one particularly interesting session, a woman was so impressed with my accuracy and the information I gave her that she gave me more than my price. When I asked why she wanted to give me more money, she told me that I was worth much more than I charge and she didn't feel right giving me less than she was about to!

Once in a while, I will go to a client's home when there are several people who want a session with me, and on one such time, I mentioned to a woman that I had a vision where she was no longer close to her father and that it appeared that she hadn't spoken to him in a long time. She confirmed to me that it had indeed been about six or seven years since she had spoken to her father. I mentioned to her that this would soon change, and that it was important for her to resume contact. I told her that maybe her father wasn't too well health-wise, and that I thought this was the right time to be ready to have a conversation with him. As soon as I mentioned this to her, she received a text message on her phone. She excused herself, saying that she was waiting for something and that she wanted to check her messages. She then looked at me and said, "I don't believe this. This is beyond anything I could understand. It's my dad." It was an extraordinary set of circumstances, not a coincidence, that this played out the way it did.

Another time, Cecile came to see me. While in session, Cecile (who is very spiritual), noticed a circle of light in my hands. She saw the circle of light in my palms due to my stigmata and hence where light comes out to fight sickness, pain and demons. She was astonished to see the light.

On another occasion, a mother of seven came to see me. I was able to see that she would be having an operation soon. She confirmed that she was scheduled for one. I told her not to do it, as she might die on the operating table, and even if she lived, she would have issues and be hospitalized a while with severe complications. Six months later, I got a message from her, telling me she wished she had listened to me. She had been months in hospital after an operation, and she almost died on the operating table. She had severe complications and they still weren't sure she would survive for sure.

She will, but regrets going through all of that.

Recently, a woman was in my office, and I began to tell her about a vision I had of a man whom I was able to describe to her, and who would approach her husband soon to make a business deal. I told her that this was a man they both knew. I mentioned that if they invested, they would lose it all. Shortly after, she messaged me telling me that I saved them a significant amount of money. Someone they had met before (who was as I described but it didn't dawn on her at the time) approached her and her husband to invest a huge amount of money in a big business venture.

Another time, a very old Italian lady came to see me. I was having a difficult day from pain in my hands and feet due to stigmata. The circles of light in my hands were powerful. The lady looked at me and said, "I know what you have. I know. I see it. Your hands, how you walk, the light around you. I met Padre Pio, the famous priest canonized by the Vatican when I was a little girl. He had stigmata. I see in you what I saw in him." That afternoon, I was able to give her an amazing clairvoyant session.

14

CONTACT OF THE DECEASED SESSIONS

It's natural to grieve the loss of a loved one. To no longer be with someone you love in the physical world is one of life's toughest challenges, and no one is immune from this loss. Death is the end, or is it?

Belief in an afterlife has been around for thousands of years, as far back as the Ancient Egyptians, 5,000 years ago. Today, we are still being led to believe by the scientific community that there is no such thing as an afterlife. After all, if we can't prove there is one, if we can't see it, touch it or hear it, then it simply can't exist. But much has changed over the last few decades about our knowledge of the afterlife. With access to the world wide web, we have so many opportunities to explore this subject. Many thousands, if not millions, of people have experienced and documented their near death experience (NDE), and they can't all be wrong. There is even a research foundation that has been established to document NDEs. (Anything you ever wanted to know about NDEs can be found at www.nderf.org.). Even though the evidence of an afterlife exists without question by those who have experienced an NDE, and their experience has affected them so much so that it has changed their outlook on life tremendously and they no longer fear death, could it all just be an illusion, a cruel hallucination? Many skeptics, and this includes most of the scientific community, think so.

There is still so much about the mind and consciousness that we don't understand. In fact, our knowledge is truly in its infancy. Scientists are now starting to believe that our brain is not our consciousness, but rather that our brain is simply a conduit for our consciousness. Our consciousness, or our soul, holds all the lessons and learnings of this life, as well as of all of our past lives.

How else can we explain the phenomena that is an NDE? A recurring event in an NDE is a person viewing their lifeless body from above a room, and coming back to tell us what the doctors and staff were saying and doing, sometimes in different rooms altogether! It's quite apparent that our consciousness is an entity apart from our physical self, and we are only beginning to grasp what this could truly mean about our understanding of spirits and the afterlife.

What if you knew that your loved ones are always with you, from the other side, helping to bring you comfort as you go about your life? What if you knew that they are in a wonderful place and they don't want you to grieve for them? What if you could tell them something you might have left unsaid while they were still alive? Wouldn't it be wonderful if it were possible for them to hear you tell them now? Well, it's not only possible, I want to tell you that you can do it every day, on your own, with no outside assistance. Your loved ones are with you always. You can speak to them anytime through your thoughts, or you can speak to them out loud if you prefer. Either way, they see and hear you. They also feel your pain. I know this is all true because I have been in contact with deceased loved ones on hundreds of occasions. The only difference between you and I is that I can hear what they wish to communicate back to you.

As crippling as the grieving process can be, a Contact of the Deceased session could strengthen (or renew) your faith in the immortality of the soul. It could help to remind you that death is not the end of life. Life simply continues in the spiritual world. A loved one's personality and character live on forever, and you will most likely see them again in spirit.

There is no doubt that many life experiences can make us question our faith, and losing a loved one is one such example. When I contact your loved one in spirit, and hear things that I could not possibly know about your loved one, then pass this information along to you, it can certainly help change your perspective. You don't need me to speak to your deceased loved ones, as you can do this yourself every day, anytime, anywhere, but if you want to know what your loved one wants to tell you, I can pass these messages on to you. These powerful sessions are usually very emotional as my clients can really sense that their loved one is there with them. After a session, many clients report a renewed faith in the afterlife. Connecting with your loved one can bring a tremendous sense of relief to those who are grieving.

Contact of the deceased sessions are my second most requested service, and I have had the honour and privilege of facilitating this communication between those in the physical world with those in the spirit realm for many years. And I don't give vague information. I have a successful session 19 times out of 20. (If I can't get a clear connection with a deceased loved one's spirit, I let my client(s) know, and they aren't charged for my service).

I'm always able to provide details to a client, things that I couldn't possibly know. In fact, when someone books an appointment with me, one of the first things I tell them is I do not want to know who they want to contact. They will only tell me the person's name when they sit down with me. We need to forget the nonsense we see in the movies, on TV, that we read in books or on the Internet, where spirits are apparently flying around and hundreds of them are ready to talk. I always contact a specific spirit, and I ask clients to bring me one of two things, or both: a picture of the person (and it can be an old picture, even a picture of them as a baby), because a picture has a residue of energy; and/or an object that they owned or was important to them, because again, there is this residue of energy which helps me to contact them. I don't need these items to make a connection with a deceased spirit, but let's face it, there are tens, if not hundreds of billions of souls in heaven, so to find one specific soul, it helps to have these tools. Generally, when I call a spirit, they appear within 3 to 5 seconds.

People have come to see me to connect with those who have passed on after being sick, or who have committed suicide, including parents of children who have passed on. Needless to say, every session is a uniquely personal one. I am able to come up with exact expressions that the deceased loved one would say to the person in front of me. I can tell them exactly how they might have dressed, their favourite foods, favourite activities - things that would be impossible for me to know and a one in a million chance for me to guess. I'm not in the guessing game.

Contact of the deceased sessions are deeply powerful and emotional. When clients begin to realize that their loved one in spirit is really there with them, and they can communicate with them and say the things that were maybe left unsaid, it becomes a life-changing experience. It's a good idea to have a list of questions that you would like to ask your loved one before our session, and I encourage you to take notes.

One such session that will forever be etched in my memory was of a father who was a police officer, who came with his son. Another of the father's sons had died in his 30s of a disease. Both the father and son in my office were extremely skeptical of me. I had spoken to the son, the brother of the child who had passed on prior to our meeting, and he acknowledged that they both believed that there might be a possibility that I could connect with his spirit, but they doubted it. The son said, "We're leaving the door open to this. We've heard good things about you and we will see if you can actually connect with him."

As the session progressed, I was able to tell them what the deceased son's favourite food was, which was fish. Now, for me anyway, I would have preferred a good pizza, or good hamburger, chicken wings, or a good poutine! There are so many other things a person could list as a favourite meal as opposed to fish, and I was able to get even more specific, and see that it was salmon. The father and son couldn't believe I was given this information.

I further saw the deceased son riding a skateboard, being into music and playing a guitar, along with other specific activities he enjoyed, and was able to give details of his facial expressions, his body language, and certain things he used to say. In fact, the connection was so good that I was able to pick up on all of this and more. This particular session stays with me because a father and a brother, who were both very skeptical, were in total disbelief. They mentioned to me that I knew things that were known just in their family, that even people close to their family didn't know. They ended up creating a video aimed at the police department to use my services. The father and son have now become some of my biggest supporters, and they have referred me many, many clients.

During various sessions, I've been able to see events that people attended, trips they had taken, where they took them, restaurants where they ate, how they died, even those who committed suicide.

Here is another typical example of a skeptic becoming a believer. A woman came to see me recently to contact her deceased loved one. Her soul mate had passed away, and she had a lot of unanswered questions. A textbook case skeptic, she had heard good things about me, and thought, "Well, if this is all baloney, at least I'll have an hour of entertainment." Of course, I knew nothing about who she wanted to contact before our session, nor her relationship with the deceased. She sat down and handed me a photo of the man she had loved, and told me his name. I summoned his spirit, and within seconds, he appeared to me. I began to describe him a little so that we could be sure we had the right person. Once that was confirmed, I was able to tell my client so much about his life; little details that I could not possibly have known. How many children he had, and the circumstances of his children's lives, which my client was able to confirm were facts.

I told her what kind of person he was, the motorcycle accident he had had, his tattoos, and other personal things. She was so moved by the experience, that she forgot to ask her questions. A few months later, she came back for another session so she could get those answers she was seeking, and sure enough, she did. Like many of my clients who come to see me to contact their deceased loved ones, she no longer had any doubt about the afterlife, and she knew she would see him again. This is why I love skeptics! She became a believer.

Another time, a woman came for a session to contact her husband who had passed away. I saw that he was murdered and that he was involved in criminal activities. I even saw who killed him and described the guy. The woman said that was who she thought it was, and that this man had since been killed.

A young man came to see me about his friend who died. I saw that his friend had committed suicide and even saw exactly how. I also saw a note he seemed to write to the girl whom he loved, and that seemed to be the main reason why he killed himself. Nobody but his family knew if there was such a note, but my client said most who knew him felt there may have been one.

Another client, a local Italian comedian, was very skeptical but he wanted to contact his mother who had passed away when he was very young. I told him things that were so deep in his subconscious that he had forgotten them. He became a believer fast!

One evening back in 2014, I heard a voice in my head and realized soon enough who was reaching out to me. It was none other than Robin Williams himself. I spoke to him before the media and the public even knew he had passed. He came to me minutes after he died. I thought I was dreaming.

HEAVEN'S MESSENGER

When I asked how he could be speaking to me, he answered that he had killed himself. I asked him why he did that, when he made so many others happy; he answered that he couldn't be happy himself. For a few minutes, he allowed me to feel how he felt just before he died. I felt a little of how he had felt, and I don't wish this pain on anyone. I asked Robin why he chose to talk to me, or why he would want to speak with anyone, period. He replied that as he crossed over, he saw a light below. I was the light that he saw and he knew we needed to chat. It was quite the honour and privilege for me. I am also certain that we will speak again.

15

CLEARING HAUNTED HOMES

The third most popular service I offer is clearing homes of entities or what I refer to as being a Haunted House Specialist. Again, due to the popularity of movies and TV shows with ghosts, people are becoming more aware of the possibility that entities may be present in their home. Haunted homes are quite common; more than most people realize. The average person will ignore the signs. They will pretend they did not see or hear certain things. They prefer to stay in their "reality as they know it" and only when it gets too chaotic in the home, will they act on it. More and more people are contacting me to cleanse their homes.

I've been to hundreds of haunted homes, offices and other locations. Each location has intrigued me, unnerved me, and reinforced my belief that good always prevails. I've witnessed people being thrown down the stairs, seen heavy furniture and cabinets being picked up and thrown across the room or even float across a room. It's very common to see pictures, mirrors, and crosses flying off walls in haunted homes. Individuals are often harassed and attacked, very often while they sleep. For these individuals sharing a space with one or more evil entities, it is usually a very unsettling experience, one which will not get better without intervention. In the majority of haunted homes I have been called to, demons, or evil spirits, are possessing either the home or a person's body.

Ghosts, which are simply souls that are stuck here in the physical realm, need to be guided to cross over to the spirit realm where they belong. Ghosts are, however, not as common as most people think. The majority of ghosts are good, not bad. When someone sees an image of a spirit, they are usually seeing a ghost.

Not long ago, I was asked to assess an old home in downtown Montreal for entities. The Notman House, a stately mansion built in the early 1840s, had a storied past. First inhabited by wealthy businessmen, it became a hospital for people deemed incurable for nearly a century. The hospital was recently relocated to Westmount, and the Notman House has now become a business centre. Over the years, rumours started swirling about the Notman House being haunted, and on a warm fall day, I set out with the crew from the morning show on the Beat 92.5, a well-known radio station in Montreal, to tour the home. It was just before Halloween, and the group from the radio station had decided that they were going to spend the night at the Notman House, as a publicity stunt. They brought in two mediums to tour the home with them and offer an expert opinion as to whether the mansion was in fact haunted. I was the second medium to tour the home. The first medium, who claimed to be able to do what I do, came in with fancy equipment and took a tour of each room, on each floor, where his equipment was able to detect fluctuations in energy that could be interpreted as evil spirits or ghosts. Now, anyone off the street can detect energy in a home with this fancy machine. It's very easy, because what are entities, ghosts, demons, and other spirits? They're energy. When you get an influx of energy and you have a machine that detects energy, it becomes very obvious where entities are. I use only my hands and my eyes. I don't use any fancy tools or equipment, such as infrared cameras or sound devices.

This event was being live-streamed on the radio station's Facebook page, and as I toured the rooms with the crew, many people began commenting about how shocked they were to see me pointing out where entities were, in the exact same locations as the previous medium had indicated with his fancy machine. In fact, it turns out that he missed a few of them!

We discovered that the Notman House is inhabited by hundreds of ghosts, spirits, and especially demons. I was able to see things with my mind that had happened there; brutal scenes of torture and people being burned alive. It was most unpleasant. The energy I could feel was completely insane, and very negative. In fact, I recall feeling this energy the moment I stepped foot in the front door. The hair on my arms stood up. There was an entity in every room I went into, and in some rooms, there were several. Suffice it to say that it's probably the one place I've been to that had the most entities, the most evil beings. I wasn't scared, as this is what I do for a living, but it was disturbing to see the amount and type of entities that were inhabiting this place. Some were so evil and so powerful. Even the crew that was with me could sense that things were 'off.'

The Notman House has many, many rooms on three floors. In one particular room we stepped into, I mentioned that there was an old woman staring at us from a chair in the corner, and one of the crew mentioned that the chair wasn't there when they passed through the home the first time around. Everyone was visibly shaken. There were so many demons in there, and demons are nothing but evil. Everyone could feel the evil presence.

Obviously, some haunted homes are inhabited by a ghost, not by evil spirits. Ghosts are generally not evil. That being said, they can cause trouble and negatively affect the home's other occupants. A ghost is usually suffering, and needs to be helped to cross over. Even if it's a friendly ghost that resides with you, it's best to help it cross over to the spirit realm where it belongs.

Following are some of the more interesting haunted homes I've been to in the past several months:

I got a call in the middle of the night, and was told that a 100-lb. cabinet in a bedroom lifted up, flew across the room, and smashed into a wall. I immediately went to the home where I saw dozens of demons. I was able to destroy them all, and found a porthole, a door open to the spirit realm right over the bedroom. I successfully closed the porthole.

A lady was seeing shadows and hearing noises in her home and asked me to clear her home of the entities. The morning of the day I was going to her home, she opened a closet door to get dressed and go to work and one of the entities whispered to her. She was able to clearly hear it say, "I know he is coming. Will you miss me when I'm gone?"

A woman had just given birth, and an entity in her home was obviously jealous. When she came back from the hospital with the newborn, she found vomit on her bed and blood on the walls. I successfully cleared the home.

For one client, I cleared her home, performed an exorcism and contacted a deceased loved one. She began to tell me that weird things were happening in her house. Her sister-in-law, who was visiting her, was unable to sleep in her room. Also, her kids wouldn't go into certain rooms; they were hearing strange noises. I went over to the house and cleared the home. There was even a ghost bartender behind the antique bar she had recently purchased. I crossed the ghost over to the spirit world. I don't destroy ghosts; I cross them over because they are physical beings stuck here in the physical world. In essence, I saved him. I noticed that my client also had a demon attached to her and I pointed to her shoulder and said so. She replied that she had been feeling very 'off' and had been experiencing pain in that shoulder for no apparent reason. I removed it and she said the pain was instantly gone. She then booked an appointment with her sister to contact their father who had passed on. It was very emotional and I told them both things that were intimate and only they could have known.

16

SHAMANIC SESSIONS

The following services that I offer are requested less frequently because there are other traditional methods that most people will try first. When these traditional methods fail, it is then that people will seek out alternative sources.

The Oxford English Dictionary describes a shaman as *a person regarded as having access to, and influence in, the world of good and evil spirits, especially among some peoples of northern Asia and North America. Typically, such people enter a trance state during a ritual, and practice divination and healing.* Shamans are highly regarded in Africa as well.

A shaman is a medicine person. Different native tribes and indigenous peoples throughout the world all have their own form of medicine person, or shaman. Shamans are known for their non-traditional work with natural herbs, foods and plants. They call it non-traditional medicine, however, shamans have been doing this for thousands of years.

There are seven levels of shaman, with seven being the highest level, and it is here where he or she goes beyond the physical treatments, and is able to connect with the spirit world, to help them help others with sickness, disease, and other ailments. I am at the seventh level. As a seventh level shaman, I am able to connect with the spiritual world, and tap into the energy from heaven to help those with pain and sickness. Some shamans connect with their relatives who have passed on, others say it's the old chiefs of the tribe who passed on; others claim to connect with animal spirits. Some like me can connect with animal spirits as well as human spirits and angels, and are able to help animals as well as people. Most shamans use plants and other forms of nature to help heal.

Very few are born naturally as shamans, as I am. I never needed to take a course. I simply needed to explore, understand and develop my gift. Some (although very few) can reach the highest level of shaman without being born into it, and they often spend 30 to 40 years in training. Most shamans reach the other levels, but usually not the highest, and they can spend 20 or more years in the jungle and/or mountains learning. It took me six months to develop my shamanic abilities as it coincided with the rest of my gift. I am still learning, of course, every day.

More and more people are turning to shamans and natural healers, often out of desperation, having achieved no success with so-called traditional medicine and treatments. The problem for people seeking a shaman is how to find a true practitioner. Unfortunately today, anyone off the street can claim to be a healer or shaman. Nonsense courses are offered now so anyone with enough money to spend can take a course for a week and think they are a real shaman. I learned about shamanism by practicing connecting with heaven and then properly becoming a vessel for the energy to be transferred to those in need of my help. I did learn about plants and ointments and creams, some of which I now make myself. Of course, I studied the human body as well.

In my shamanic treatments, the physical element does play a part, because the energy comes through my hands, and I use my hands to help people, but that's the only physical element. There are no machines, no fancy treatment, no medication, no herbs or spices. I will often suggest certain foods or certain plants to help my clients, absolutely. I'm a firm believer in the power of nature. I have a deep connection with Mother Earth, and spend a lot of time in nature, either in a forest or near a body of water. Being near the ocean or in a forest is very powerful. I am blessed to have a forest in my backyard where I have a deep affinity with the native wildlife and birds.

Helping people with disease, sickness and pain is only part of the shamanic services I offer. I also offer a chakra treatment (chakra being the Hindu word for energy point of the body). Chakras are the main energy centres of the body, and they get emotional and spiritual blockages. Just as the body can have physical issues, we can get spiritual and emotional blockages as well. I offer a very deep shamanic chakra treatment. Very often, this includes psychology as we need to face certain aspects of our life and let go, to end these blockages. I give an energy treatment where heavenly energy flows from above, through me, to my hands, and then to the person on my massage table. I very often use a shamanic oil blend, an organic blend that I make myself, and very often, I use hot stones.

Each chakra is associated with a specific colour, like a rainbow, and in effect, they are the same colours as a rainbow. People have been able to see the different colours swirling around in their mind as I work to open the chakras. Clients have been able to feel the energy from my hands, even when my hands were a foot or more above their body. People have said to me, "I don't know if I'm crazy, but as you're working on opening my chakras, I think I see Jesus." Or, "I think I see Moses, or Mary," or even "I see the angels as if they were standing right here next to you, next to me."

Clients have had incredible experiences on my table. One particularly interesting session was of a woman who not only saw the colours clearly, and felt my energy (she said that my energy was permeating throughout her entire body), she felt a pulse, or vibration, as I was working on her. I was ending the session with hot stones, as I often do, that I had energized myself with my hands. This helps to balance and align the chakras once they're opened, and make them in harmony with each other. I always tell my clients that when the chakras are in harmony, working together, very often people can feel their heart beat in some of the stones, especially the one near the bottom, what I call the base chakra at the bottom of the spine or top of the buttocks. Well, with this particular individual, not only did the hot stone at the base of the spine have a vibration that she knew was her heart beat, but it was so intense, it started pulsating on her back and vibrating so intensely and powerfully, the hot stone actually hopped off her back. That's how intense the session was! This is how powerful it can become when I give this energy treatment to open and balance the chakras.

As a shaman, people come to see me with lots of different ailments: pain, sickness, cancer, colitis, depression, anxiety, joint issues, arthritis – the list goes on and on. One young lady, in her thirties, suffered tremendous pain for 11 years. She couldn't take two steps without her feet and legs being in terrible pain. She had tried doctors and traditional medicine, physiotherapy, and other treatments. She had lost hope. Nothing helped her in those 11 years. She came to see me with tears in her eyes, begging me to help ease her pain, and five treatments was all it took for her to become completely pain-free. In fact, a few days after our last treatment together, she took part in a charity event; a walk to raise money for disease. She walked five kilometres to raise money for this event. She went from not being able to take two steps without being in excruciating pain, to walking five kilometres. I'm also happy to report that two years later, she is still pain-free. It was a special experience for me to be able to help such a wonderful lady, especially at such a young age, who didn't want to do anything or go anywhere because of the pain. In some ways, she was given her life back. Not long after, her boyfriend called me crying. He was in unbelievable pain and was lying on the floor, unable to move. I drove over to his home and was able to remove enough pain for him to be able to get up off the floor.

An 80-year-old European man came to see me for a shamanic treatment recently. His daughter had put him in contact with me. The old man was going blind. Already legally blind, it was getting worse. If you put your hand more than six inches away from his face, he could just see the outline or a little shadow. I explained to him before we started the session that there are never any guarantees. I did get the impression from the angels above though, that I would be able to help him in a small way, but it would not be a complete success. I knew I could not reverse it, but that I could make a significant improvement to his eyesight. This man was seeing his doctor once a month and getting needles in his eyes to prevent his eyesight from worsening. I mentioned that I could most likely improve his eyesight by 5%, and he looked at me and said, "Listen, even a 1% improvement would make a world of difference for me, so please go ahead."

After five or six treatments, I was able to put my hand about ten feet away from his face and he could see it. He was thrilled, and when he went back to the doctor to get his shots, the doctor told him (after testing his vision), that his eyesight seemed to have gotten a little better. The doctor couldn't believe this because the shots the man was getting were only to prevent his eyesight from getting worse. There was no chance that his eyesight could improve, and here the doctor was seeing an improvement. He found this incredible to witness.

Sheila came to me for a chakra treatment. After I opened up and balanced the body's energy points, Sheila said it was the most powerful experience energy-wise that she had ever had and she could see light surrounding me. She is extremely spiritual and is an expert at meditation, as well as being a well-known yoga instructor. Sheila had such an amazing experience, that she brought an ex-boyfriend to see me whom she knew was possessed. She could sense the demon and had witnessed him growling at people, speaking in foreign tongue, and had black eyes all the time. During the exorcism, she swears that she could actually see the light shooting out of my hands and attacking the demon! After these two experiences, she brought her new boyfriend to me. He had been in a motorcycle accident and had some severe injuries, along with trouble using one arm due to shoulder and wrist injuries. I gave him one shamanic treatment and he was blown away to the point of tears. He swears he saw Jesus while I was working on him and could see light around me. He was also able to feel the energy through his entire body; an incredible warmth and beautiful feeling.

Not long after that session, the couple's dog got very sick with kidney failure. The veterinarian didn't give the dog long to live. They brought the animal to me and in one session, I was able to help her. She jumped off my table and was running around my backyard. At the next visit to the veterinarian, the vet said it was unbelievable to see her like that!

Another animal I was able to help was a client's horse. Her horse had had a bad fall, and vets thought they would need to put the horse down. I worked on the horse and the next day, he was better. The vets couldn't believe it.

A woman came to see me for a chakra treatment. The last chakra I work on is called the crown chakra which is known to be the direct connection to the light, to the Creator. While I was working on the crown chakra, my client was lying on the table, and she looked at me in shock and said, "Am I crazy or is that Jesus standing next to you, and angels, actual angels flying around you and I?" She was not crazy!

17

EXORCISMS

In the U.S. alone, over the past ten years, the number of official priest exorcists has more than quadrupled, and two of America's most active exorcists have stated that it is an ongoing struggle to keep up with the demand.[1]

Also, according to the Catholic News Agency (CNA), an Irish priest and exorcist by the name of Fr. Pat Collins recently began asking the country's bishops for more support after noticing a dramatic increase in demonic activity in the country. Even the International Association of Exorcists (IAE) said levels of demonic activity throughout the world had reached what they considered a "pastoral emergency."[2] It's realistic to conclude that the statistics would be similar in Canada and other parts of the world, as well.

Collins said that he was "baffled" that the bishops hadn't trained more exorcists in Ireland, and added that anyone who didn't see the need for more exorcists was "out of touch with reality."

First of all, I don't believe Catholic priests are capable of performing real exorcisms. It's not enough to have a clerical collar or to wear a black robe, to throw some holy water, or to carry a

Christian Bible. I'm not saying it's not possible for a Catholic priest to have this ability to perform an exorcism, but if this is true, there are maybe one or two in the entire world. How do I know this? Because I am an exorcist! I don't use holy water, nor do I use the Bible. I do mention the name of God by his Hebrew name (the name which most people should not be saying because it's extremely powerful). I use this name to help me in my battle. I have met humans in demon form and I see people who are possessed all the time by spiritual demons.

Now, if a demon in human form, or inside someone, can walk into a house of God, a synagogue, a church, or mosque, and stand there and pick up the Bible, whether it be the Old or the New Testament, the Torah or the Koran, be surrounded by people who are praying and chanting holy things, and not get affected at all, then how can a priest throwing some holy water be enough to perform an exorcism? It's not, and it never will be. It's that simple. A priest simply does not have this power.

They also claim that an exorcist has to be a Catholic priest, and in fact, these priests need to be part of some organization that's recognized by the Vatican, as if the Vatican can speak for all of humanity, all 7.5 billion people on earth! As if the Vatican is the only organization that has the right to tell people what to do and how to do it. That only a Catholic, and only one sponsored by the Vatican, who holds a certificate from the Vatican that allows him to be an official exorcist on their behalf, only they are able to do the work of God! This is complete hogwash and nonsense!

I know there are very few real exorcists in the world who can perform an actual exorcism, yet according to the Catholic religion, there are 50-60 priests in the U.S. alone who are capable of doing so. They also claim that there are tens of thousands of people coming to them every year. Now, there are a lot of people who are possessed, absolutely, but their numbers are way off. They also claim that of all the people who come to them, that maybe only five or ten people are actually possessed. Those numbers are actually much higher. These priests wouldn't know a demon if it fell out of the sky and hit them on the head, or if one came from below and crawled up their leg. Nor would they truly understand someone who is possessed unless it was a very severe case, like someone climbing up the walls, or speaking in tongue while the eyes turn black and black gunk starts coming out of their mouth. These are obvious cases.

Some of the other claims are that unless you are a Catholic priest, it's dangerous to perform exorcisms. I think it's the opposite! It's dangerous to let a Catholic priest perform an exorcism! When you look at some of their methods, very often, a priest will start beating the person, as if beating the physical body will get the demon out. This is complete nonsense! They also claim that if someone has a mental illness, it's dangerous to perform an exorcism on such a person. My question to them is this: How would they even know if someone has a mental illness? What qualifies them to decide who is possessed, and who has a mental illness? The Catechism of the Catholic Church emphasizes the importance of distinguishing between demonic activity and mental illness. Before a Catholic priest or exorcist can perform an exorcism, mental illness must first be ruled out. If the rite of exorcism is still needed, they may seek out a priest who has been trained and appointed as exorcist by his bishop, including practicing exorcists, medical professionals, psychologists, lawyers and theologians. Unfortunately, many people seeking exorcisms by means of the Catholic church fall between the cracks and are often not helped, according to Fr. Collins.[2]

What if someone has a mental illness and is possessed? What happens then? I do know if someone has a mental illness or is possessed. How? Because I can see what's inside someone. There are people who come to me who legitimately have a mental disease and I see that there is no demon, and I tell them that they are not possessed.

I have met a lot of Catholic priests, and I do believe that most of them are wonderful people, and those who claim to be exorcists actually believe what it is they're saying. They are decent people who believe what the Vatican has told them; they believe in what the pope has told them, they believe in the Catholic ideology and they believe that they're making a difference and helping people. Unfortunately, this is not the case.

At the time of this writing, I've performed four exorcisms in just the past week, two of which were on young children. Three of these four exorcisms were in advanced stages of demonic possession, where the person's free will was almost completely gone. Of all the different entities out there, contrary to popular belief, demons are the most common. Demons are not to be ignored, because they won't simply go away. You can't just tell them to leave; they must be destroyed.

Some of the more interesting and hellish exorcisms that I've performed are on children. More than half of those who come to see me or who are brought to me by others are children. Some are as young as four or five years old. Children are pure and innocent - and gullible - and this is why they are so vulnerable. Evil likes to go after those who are vulnerable, which makes children ideal targets. At the other end of the spectrum, I've performed an exorcism on an individual over 80 years of age.

I have seen and done a great deal of exorcisms. I've had parents call me because one of their children picked them up and tossed them across the room. On another occasion, a distressed woman called to tell me that she had woken up in the middle of the night to see her son leaning over her and touching her inappropriately. He had dark eyes and was speaking in deep voice and had a smile on his face as he was touching her. He asked her, "Do you like that, mommy?" She came to see me with her son, and when they stepped into my office, the little boy looked at a painting I have hanging on the wall of Jesus that an eight-year-old girl had painted years ago. The image of Jesus is very much as He appears to me. This painting of Jesus doesn't look anything like what most people imagine Him to look like, with the beard and long white robe. Most people have no idea who the person is in the painting, but this boy knew exactly who He was right away and proceeded to spit on the painting, and laugh at the picture. He then sat on the floor, spread out his arms and legs, and said, "Yeah, it was me who put the nails in His hands and feet on the Cross."

It was an intense session which required many hours of work on this little boy to rid him of the demon inside. This demon was one of the most powerful ones I have encountered. I'm happy to say that I won this battle through the help from above, and when we were finished, the boy got down on his knees and started crying. He began praying in front of the painting on the wall, and asking Jesus to forgive him for what he had said and done when he wasn't in control.

Someone who is possessed is used to having that demon inside them and is actually sad when it leaves their body. You could compare this to a withdrawal from drugs, or other substance. One little girl I was able to help began to cry after the demon left, and I asked her why she was crying. She said, "It's gone. The voices are gone. Who am I going to talk to now? Who will tell me what I should do now?" It was heartbreaking to see, even though we all felt better that the demon was gone. It's just one of the side effects of demonic possession.

These are only some of the severe cases I've seen. I went to a home where I found a child hanging from the chandelier, with a loaded gun in his hand. I've seen many crazy things and have had many wild experiences. I get threatened all the time during exorcisms; demons tell me that they are going to kill me and my family, tell me that they are going to rape my wife, or my daughter, and all kinds of other nasty things that demons love to say because that's how disgusting they are. They swear at me and they threaten me all the time, yet I am used to it. It's just part of my job.

Possession is very real. Some who are possessed can be directed by a demon to hurt themselves or even kill themselves or other people. There are different levels of possession, and though some cases are not as severe, I do consider all possessions to be serious. People with full-fledged powerful demonic possessions are not in control of their bodies. There are also bad spirits who take over people's bodies, not necessarily demonic spirits, however, I am usually dealing with demons as they are much more powerful.

Some exorcisms are less extreme; people will simply twitch while I perform the exorcism. It's not like what you may have seen on TV or in the movies, where a possessed person's head spins around (after all, if a head did spin around, the body would die, and the demon wants the body). What I do see, however, are growling, the black eyes, things coming out of the mouth, including black 'gunk' (or guck) as I call it, the deep voice, speaking in Latin and/or foreign tongue. These are all things I have witnessed on more than one occasion.

Here are some more client experiences:

The mother of a 6-year-old boy called to tell me that her son had picked her up with one hand and had thrown her down the stairs. And at school, he ripped up his test paper, gave his teacher the finger and in a deep voice, told the teacher to go fuck herself. I don't lose battles with demons and I'm able to help all those possessed who come to me for help.

A woman called me and told me that her 10-year-old daughter stabbed her sister with a pen, was constantly talking to herself, always had an evil smirk and was swearing all the time. At one point during the exorcism, the demon wouldn't let her talk, so she drew me a picture of herself chained and unable to speak or see. I performed a successful exorcism. When I was done, the girl was crying. Her mother asked her why she was crying, and the girl said that she was sad because I took the voice out of her head, that I had killed it and she was lonely and no longer had anybody to talk to.

A man's girlfriend call me. He was speaking a foreign language he never learned, his eyes were black, and he was threatening to kill himself and her. He came into my office swearing at me, and telling me the devil was stronger than my boss. Black gook was coming out of his mouth while I was fighting the demon. Three people, including his girlfriend, witnessed me perform the exorcism, and when I was done, the man smiled and laughed, at which point the others all said it was the first time he had laughed in six months.

An 80-year-old reiki master called me. He had seen an article about me in the newspaper, and told me that he felt only I could help him. He got possessed performing reiki (energy work) on clients, and he was the sweetest, kindest man, but he was fighting a demon that he knew he couldn't beat. He was in my office with his wife, and he mentioned to me that he was losing the battle; he was swearing, had a threatening demeanor, eyes shifting, deep voice, etc. I performed a successful exorcism, and he promised to stop doing reiki, even though he had been practicing it for 35 years.

Another client needed an exorcism and a home cleared of entities. This lady claimed to do everything I could do, but admitted that she was possessed and needed help. And as I am more powerful than anyone else she knew, she asked me to go over to her house. When I entered the home, I saw entities everywhere. I killed them all and the whole time, she was shaking, swearing, eyes shifting and changing colours. When I was finished clearing her home, she began cursing and threatening to hurt me; her boyfriend had to hold her down on the sofa. I performed a successful exorcism. She passed out, then woke up feeling fine.

Another client drove several hours from the U.S. to see me. Nobody had been able to help her: the Catholic church had even sent exorcists with no luck. In my office, the demon was using her to taunt me, saying that I couldn't win. Every time the woman tried to think of God, it caused her pain and she would twitch and squirm, cry and moan. It took three hours to fight this demon. She was able to feel the light working through her. Once again, I did what needed to be done during the exorcism.

A man came to see me who was possessed. I performed a successful exorcism and a week later, he texted me to say that the only way to describe how he was feeling was to say that he felt protected, like there was a shield of light around him now.

A large man, a 6'2" bodybuilder, muscular and strong, called me and told me that he woke up the previous night unable to breathe. He felt that some things were holding him down and choking him. He couldn't breathe or get these things off of him. He said his bed was shaking from all that action. I went to see him and noticed that he had several demons attached to him. I was able to help him.

How do people get possessed? There are a variety of ways possession can happen. For one thing, it's important to be careful about meditation. When you meditate, you open the door to spirits and demons into your life. Also, using Ouija boards is a sure way to invite bad spirits into your life. Stay away from people who use them as well. Group meditations are particularly bad; I would never participate in a group meditation for this reason.

Those who dabble in black magic and the occult, who think it would be fun to talk to evil spirits, can get possessed. Evil spirits and demons are very smart and cunning. They trick you into thinking they are good spirits. The average person cannot determine a good spirit from a bad spirit. Some people cannot even determine right from wrong. Even most mediums cannot tell the difference between good and evil because they are not open enough, spiritually. If people who talk to spirits on a daily basis have trouble determining good and evil, how can the average person do so?

Evil doesn't come to you with a horrible face and tell you it's going to do awful things to you and make your life a living hell; it disguises itself as a good spirit with a nice face and a smile, and it tells you that it wants to help you and give you nice things, and improve your life. All you have to do is let the spirit in, and it promises to give you everything you want. It pretends to be your friend. And the average person will allow them to enter into their life because they cannot see the evil behind the facade. One thing is certain: Nothing can possess you unless you allow it to. You cannot get possessed without giving your permission.

MENTAL ILLNESS AND POSSESSION

I have helped many clients with anxiety and depression, both of which are forms of mental illness. The brain is like a computer and sometimes the connection is not right or the energy is all over the place. I am no doctor, psychologist or psychiatrist nor am I trying to be. Nor am I meant to replace them or any other healthcare professional in their respective fields. The following is my opinion only. Yes, mental illness is real. What is also real is the fact that anyone claiming to hear voices or that the devil speaks to them or that they want to harm others or themselves is automatically treated as someone with a mental illness and is treated with medication. Again, I am no expert on mental illness. I am an expert on demons and demonic possession, however, and one of the few in the world who can perform a legitimate exorcism. I will say that not all people who have been diagnosed with mental disease are sick or have mental illness. Many are not. Many are possessed. One of the more common signs of someone who is possessed is wanting to hurt themselves or others. Another is certainly hearing voices and thinking the devil is talking to them. Of course, as soon as they tell that to a medical professional it is presumed they have mental illness. What if they don't? Will medication help them? Certainly not.

It may be a good idea for people to think outside the box on this issue. Medication and locking someone up in a mental institution will not help someone who is possessed. How do medical professionals explain someone whose eyes turn black and speak in foreign tongue and deeper voices, or the bodies contort into non-recognizable things? In fancy terms of course!

Or the famous so-called "unknown reason." There are medical professionals who are willing to admit a miracle has happened when someone gets healed out of nowhere or unexpectedly. Why can't more people in the mental illness field open up to other possibilities and solutions as well? There are some well known psychiatrists and psychologists who are open-minded and even some who openly admit and discuss mental illness and demonic possession and the possible link between the two, as well as believing that most people in mental facilities are not sick, but actually possessed.

Take, for instance, Richard Gallagher, a certified psychiatrist, who also works as an adjunct professor in the Department of Clinical Psychiatry at the New York Medical College, who says that mental illness stems from demonic possession. This is a first in the world of psychiatry, as most medical practitioners who speak of anything deemed a fringe topic by the mainstream, automatically jeopardize both their careers and practice. According to Gallagher, he has personally encountered many patients, whom he believes are controlled by demonic possessions.[3]

Dr. Gallagher also goes on to say that it is more illogical to outright reject the existence of a spiritual world. "As a psychoanalyst, a blanket rejection of the possibility of demonic attacks seems less logical, and often wishful in nature, than a careful appraisal of the facts."[4] I support this statement 100%.

There are ways to guard yourself from becoming possessed by demonic spirits. First of all, make sure to never say yes to an entity who asks to come inside. This can happen almost anytime, whether you're awake, asleep or during meditation. Make sure to always refuse anything to come inside; even if it looks like Jesus himself! Children are vulnerable since they are pure and innocent, and gullible, and vulnerable adults are targets as well. These can include people who dabble in black magic and the occult, play with Ouija boards, and other forms of reaching out to spirits. These people should be extra vigilant.

18

MESSAGES AND LESSONS WE CAN LEARN

Life can be amazing when everything's going well, and yet we all face hurdles and setbacks. We are all here on a spiritual journey, so we need to have faith that there is something bigger and more powerful than us at work here. I call this higher power God; others may call it the source or the Creator, or the universe. Just understand that there is something bigger and more powerful than us. This higher power or source, can inspire us in good times and comfort us in times of despair.

Our lives are preplanned by divine design. Our souls are here to fulfill a mission, or purpose, and only once that's accomplished, does our soul return to the spiritual realm. Everything about our lives is predetermined, however, our situations can change anytime through the power of free will. This is why I don't believe in coincidences. Everything happens for a reason.

We also need to be open-minded. Sure, you can be skeptical, and because there are so many fakes and frauds in the spiritual industry, you should be skeptical. Being skeptical is healthy, as is being open-minded, and shows that you are not going to follow along like sheep. We should question everything. We should research everything. Close-minded people are not willing to see any other opinion or option that may be different than their own. And even when given proof that they may be wrong, they are unwilling to see it.

Evil is very real. There are many who believe that there is no such thing as evil. Evil is not only real, it has been since the beginning and will be here until that final battle between good and evil, between the light and the shadow. We should not fear evil, because good will always win. I have an incredible success record of removing demons and clearing haunted homes. I don't lose because I am a vessel for heaven, and they use me to spread the light. Heaven never loses to the shadow.

Not only is evil very real, it's very powerful. Over the last few millennia, humans have acted in such a way that has given power to evil, and as such, evil currently rules the world on the physical plane. Evil is why we are being poisoned, it's why we're being lied to left and right. Evil controls many of the organizations and tools that are used to control, manipulate and brainwash us.

Not only is evil real and powerful, it is tricky, and even the minions - the demons - are sneaky and tricky. The spiritual world can be a beautiful place. I deal with it every day. But the spirit world can also be extremely dangerous. How can we avoid evil intentions or spirits? We have five senses – seeing, hearing, smelling, tasting and touching - but we also have a sixth sense. What is a sixth sense? It's not considered a physical sense, it's a spiritual sense. It's our gut feeling, our intuition. We all have this sixth sense, and we should always listen to it.

Another lesson: prepare yourself for that final battle. It will be physical, it will be emotional, and it certainly will be spiritual. At some point, there has to be a final battle between good and evil. What's going on in the world will come to a head. Open yourself up to the possibility that some of the things you've believed your whole life might be wrong. Maybe things you have done that you thought were correct are not. Very often, the things we do feed the shadow, not the light. We need to dig deep, to know what's right or wrong, because the final battle is coming.

We are all human. It does not matter someone's religion, skin colour, background, race, creed, or sexual orientation. We all come from the same source. Our souls all come from the same place. We all bleed red. We all live on this earth together, so please don't judge, or think that one person is better than the other. What determines someone who is good or someone who is not are their actions, not how they look or how short or tall they are, skinny or fat, Christian, Hebrew or Muslim, Hindu, Sikh, atheist or Buddhist, gay, straight, bisexual, transgender, nationality - none of that matters. What matters is, are they good people or not? Are they showing kindness and trying to help others, or are they greedy and destructive? Are they trying to make a difference, or are they trying to take advantage? We are all here to spread the light, to spread goodness and kindness. To make a positive difference in someone's life, no matter what's going on in ours. Living this way also makes it very hard for evil spirits to influence us, for evil cannot take a hold of us if we don't allow it to.

One final thought. And it ties into that final battle that we must prepare for. It is not enough to sit on the sidelines. Or to not make a choice. In fact, if we do not make a choice, we are making the wrong choice. We are choosing to not be on the side of good, to not be on the side of light, and many famous people throughout history, including Albert Einstein, Dr. Martin Luther King and others before them, have said that one who stands by and allows evil to flourish is just as guilty as those committing the evil. By not intervening to stop evil, we are allowing it to continue to go undefeated.

19

FINAL THOUGHTS

I have already stated that there is no such thing as a message for all of humanity. This is true. Yet there are a few messages that we can each relate to and which would be wise for all to take into consideration. But before I get to that, I want to talk about religion vs. spirituality. It is not enough to be religious. You must put it into practice. In fact, dressing the part and knowing the part must become acting the part. Knowing the Holy Book inside out means nothing if we don't act out what we learn.

Here is what truly is important:

<u>Be kind. Be good.</u> This is the most important message in the universe. Helping others. Going out of our way to make a positive difference for people. This is what the Lord wants. So if we know the book inside out but are not good and kind, it means nothing. In fact, heaven prefers that we not be religious and instead be good and kind if we need to choose only one option. 'Do unto others as we want done unto us and do not do unto others that which we do not wish done to us' is the most important quote in the universe.

<u>We must be prepared to make choices. The right choices.</u> Most often the right choices to make are not the easy ones, but rather the tough ones. We must remember the expression "The road to hell is paved with good intentions." What we think is correct very often is not. We make many choices with the right intentions, however the choices are actually hurting and not helping the universe. This is due to many reasons but especially because of how we as a people have been conditioned and brainwashed. We have been spoon-fed what society feels is right and wrong. Go with your gut feeling. Use common sense. Think before making decisions. The time is coming when we will all be faced with important choices. Many will make the wrong choice, so be ready.

<u>Don't be so easily fooled.</u> Don't believe what the media tells you or what the education system tells you. Don't believe what the politicians tell you or what society tells you. Use your intuition. Use your common sense. Question everything. The devil does not appear with red horns and a pitchfork but rather with a smile and rainbow and a bouquet of roses. The devil and his minions are the masters of lies. Always be open-minded. Do not close yourself off into a box. Research everything you learn. Research everything you are told. Question it all! Growth and learning come from going outside our box. It comes from going out of what we know and are used to. We must get uncomfortable. We must explore the unknown. We need to go where we haven't gone before. Just because a doctor or politician or media outlet or teacher or Hollywood actor says something

does not make it so. It does not make it truth or reality. Remember as well what Mark Twain said, "I do not let my schooling get in the way of my education."

<u>Now is the time to make a difference.</u> We are all here on earth to make a difference, to leave our mark, so to speak. This is a daily task and obligation for those of us who understand we are here to help others and change lives for the better. The time to really make a difference is now. It's time to kick it into high gear. Evil is powerful right now and goodness and light must fight back with full force. Each of us must show as much goodness and kindness as possible. Each of us must help as many people as possible, including strangers. Each of us must help animals and nature. All are the Lord's creations. The time for action is now. Not tomorrow. Now. Spread the light. It is needed more than ever.

<u>We are all connected.</u> We are all human regardless of race or background or sexual orientation. We all come from the same source. We may have different physical attributes, yet we all share the same source of energy. We are all the same inside. Nobody is better than the next. It is only our actions that determine who we are. Nobody should ever be judged based on their skin colour, background, nationality, religion, social status or sexual orientation. We need to understand that we are all in this together. Don't think you are better than another because of how you grew up or your background. Do not look down on others. We share

this beautiful place called earth. Share it in peace and understanding and cooperation.

Finally, don't let those with evil intentions separate us as people. Don't buy into the us-vs.-them narrative that is created to keep us divided. Together we are amazing and can achieve anything.

Blessings,
Jarred

GLOSSARY OF SPIRITUAL DEFINITIONS

Angel: Being of light brought into being by the Creator as messengers. Angel comes from the Greek word angelos meaning messenger. Original term for angel is the Hebrew term Malach, also meaning messenger. They do God's bidding and often watch over us; hence, the term guardian angel. A guardian, a protector. They can take physical form but rarely do. Even when speaking with me they take shape in the spiritual realm only to distinguish one from the other. Each has a personality and certain physical attributes to distinguish them, such as hair, facial expressions, clothing, etc. Contrary to popular belief, angels are not our loved ones who have passed on. They are not saints either, and rarely are they human (aside from only two angels, none were ever human). Some however, have come down in human form. I have met a few. Angels will appear as having wings as it somehow makes it easier for humans to identify with them, but they do not have wings. Angels are not male or female. They have no gender. However, angels are either more masculine or more feminine. This is also due to the fact that the Creator and the entire universe is made up of both masculine and feminine energy; therefore, angels represent that.

Archangel: Same as angels, however, they would be considered the higher echelon of angels. The generals, if you will. Such names as Michael, Gabriel and Raphael make up the archangels. I work directly with them and other archangels.

Chakra: Hindu term for energy centre of the body. There are seven main chakras in the body. There are many others as well.

Clairvoyant: One who sees. Another term for psychic. Someone who can see the future.

Demon: Opposite of angel. There were two different occasions where angels fell from heaven and became known as the fallen angels or fallen ones. The devil himself was the leader of the angels who fell the second time. Demons can be in physical form walking amongst us. They can be and most often are in spiritual form. They are beings of shadow as opposed to beings of light and are created as such. There are also those born as offspring to demons and humans. Suffice it to say that demons are everything that angels are not. Demons represent everything evil and wrong with the world. Their job is to create suffering and to fight everything and anything good and kind.

Exorcist: One who performs an exorcism on a possessed body. One who removes a demon who has taken possession of a physical body. Contrary to popular belief, there are very few real exorcists alive today. One does not need to be Catholic to perform one nor to be saved by one.

Fairy: A mystical creature, also real. Fairies are both physical and spiritual. They are playful and mischievous. They do not interfere often in our lives, but are always present, usually in nature.

Fallen Angel: Term that refers to the group of angels who fell from heaven and came to earth. They became demons as did their offspring and descendants.

Ghost: The term led to the word ghost hunter or ghost buster. A ghost is believed to be the most common form of entity. In fact, most people, including those in the spiritual field, refer to most entities as ghosts. Ghosts are actually the least common found entity. A ghost is a soul stuck in the physical world. It is a soul that never crossed into the spirit realm. In fact, it is trapped here.

Haunted House Specialist: One who can truly handle a haunted location. One who specializes in the removal of entities haunting a location.

Heaven: Heaven is not 'above.' Heaven is a beautiful place in the spirit realm that is all around us. It is the name for a place where good souls go to rest in peace and happiness.

Light: A term used to refer to a holy energy or place, like heaven. A term used to mean goodness and kindness and holiness. Opposite of shadow. The light can refer to the Creator, God. It is pure and bright. A place where darkness and shadow and therefore evil cannot reside.

Medium: A term referring to one who can connect with the deceased. Someone with the ability to speak with spirits. Often, this term is incorrectly used to also refer to psychics.

Psychics: Those who can see the future. Those who receive visions of what is to come. The word psychic often has a negative connotation.

Reiki: A form of energy work originally from Japan. People take courses on how to manipulate and use energy, supposedly to help heal others.

Reiki Master: One who reaches a high level within the reiki framework. One who teaches others reiki.

Shadow: Opposite of light. A term often used to refer to evil, the devil. A term used to refer to darkness.

Shaman: One who helps heal others. A medicine man. In fact, in aboriginal, native and indigenous peoples and tribes, each with their own version of a shaman and each with their own name for such, a shaman is usually an elder of the tribe and one who studied for decades. In most indigenous tribes throughout the world, shamans are respected and trusted. Furthermore, in many tribes, especially in the Americas, there are seven levels of shaman; Level 7 is he or she who can help heal by connecting with the spirit world.

Shape Shifters: One who can change shape. One who can become something other than its original form. Demons are often shape shifters, both in the spiritual and physical realm. The most common shape shifter is a human who can become a wolf. Those who become wolves are good and not bad, contrary to popular belief.

Spirit: A soul that has crossed over to the spirit world. Spirits can be both good or bad.

Spirit Realm: Opposite of physical world. Spirit realm has no physicality to it, nor is there time as we know it; the past, present and future happen simultaneously. The spirit realm is where souls go. It is where angels and spirits reside. It is where evil resides as well. When someone passes, their soul is meant to cross over into the spiritual world.

Stigmata: The marks and/or pain of what Jesus suffered on the Cross. Very few throughout history have ever suffered the stigmata.

Vampires: They are real. Unlike those in the movies, actual vampires are both physical and spiritual and instead of drinking and sucking blood, they suck positive energy. They are energy vampires who leave their victims drained, and often sick. They do not live forever and you cannot fight them with garlic or wooden stakes.

Werewolf: Mythical creature. A creature that is human yet can become part human and part wolf. There are those who are human yet who can become a wolf, which is different from a werewolf.

Yeshua: Hebrew name of Jesus as He was a Hebrew.

TESTIMONIALS

"Thank you Jarred, and you were right when you told me a new and creative job was around the corner. I'm a very happy camper at my new job! I couldn't have asked for a better fit on every level."
- *Melanie*

"Good morning Jarred! Thank you so much for last night. He's very tired. He fell asleep immediately after we left! He's different already, his presence is light and innocent. Not loud and heavy. He thanked me and fell asleep. God bless you, I will forever be in debt to you for what you have done for my family and I! God bless." - *Lynn*

"Well I know you're for real, you helped our family by clearing my house of spirits. There will always be people who don't believe. You have a gift and you helped me so much." - *Christina*

"Jarred did a cleansing at my house. It was necessary." - *Sandra*

"Jarred did a reading on my mom which I heard about. Everything he predicted has happened so far." - *Alexa*

"Jarred was awesome." - *Micheline*

"You have the gift...I know for sure you're the real deal, because what you said a while ago to me is happening now. Keep up the great work." - *Angie*

"I can attest 100% that Jarred is for real!" - *Greg*

"You are AWESOME! Keep up the good work." - *Joe*

"Last night after my chakra healing and balancing session with a real medium (light worker) finished, we got into a spiritual discussion and my eyes are now even wider! I love knowing truths; not residing in a zombie state and pretending all is well. What I now know makes me want to work even harder in the direction of LIGHT. Thanks a lot Jarred! You are truly what you say you are...you're a blessing to this world my darling. Blessings and Love." - *Yolanda*

"Yes, I understand your feeling of enlightenment after seeing Jarred. The aura around him - anyone spiritual can feel his light healing. His strong energy is infused by this light. You can actually feel the heat; healing penetrating into you as he massages. It's something everyone should experience. It's also a chance for a person to connect; open themselves to good; a widened Universe. Definitely a higher awareness." - Joddy

"Last night I had a wonderful clairvoyance and energy session with Jarred. He was precisely accurate in his reading of my life with answers to all my questions and a path for the future mapped out for me. After our reading he proceeded with a chakra balancing and with the opening of every chakra he guided me and gave me the confidence to face long overdue issues that were plaguing me.

"After the opening he balanced them with hot stones for 15 minutes and they say when your chakras are open and balanced you can actually feel your heartbeat in all of them and I am glad to say that I felt it in all of them. This morning I woke up refreshed and did not feel the negativity around as I had in the past. It was a wonderful experience with a gifted soul. I highly recommend to everyone. Thank you Jarred." - *Lori*

"I wanted to share my experience and give a big 'thank you' to Jarred for his kindness and beautiful gift. My reading was very accurate and his visions were really clear. He was able to connect with someone very special to me who had passed away. It was comforting to know she is happy and smiling. My energy treatment was magical. I could feel his healing energy throughout my entire treatment. I'm looking forward to when we can meet again. Thank you!" - *Cathryn*

"I really enjoyed my experience with Jarred! He did a reading for my mom and I and told us things that no one would have known! I recommend his services to everyone." - *Jessica*

"I definitely recommend it! Very emotional and touching... It was a moving experience indeed, and I would do it again." - *Peter*

"Feeling thankful to have met Jarred. I've seen him twice; first to clear my house of bad spirits that had been bothering my family. Since you came there are no more things happening or uneasy feelings. The second time was for a clairvoyant reading. The visions he saw were accurate and clear. My favourite part was when he contacted a family member that had passed and getting some comforting advice. Your abilities are a beautiful gift. Thank you for everything Jarred."
- *Cathy*

"I met with Jarred last week and received a message that gave me peace. Thank you for sharing your gift with me." - *Diane*

"Thank you Jarred. It was a peaceful experience. Thanks for answering my questions & talking with me." - *Joanne*

"I wanted to share my experience with Jarred because I truly believe he can help anyone willing to open their heart and mind to a better understanding of life. For the last couple of years I haven't been myself. Life's struggles had finally caught up to me and had taken their toll. I wasn't myself anymore; I was empty... I knew I had to do something to get myself back on track. I sought out so many different types of help but nothing worked until I met Jarred. We had crossed paths before he was the man he is today and I believe he re-entered my life with a purpose. Nothing is by chance, at my lowest point I decided to try his services and what a difference.

"Particularly in energy healing. In only one short session, what took me years of soul searching, it all finally clicked! Clarity at last! I finally feel like myself again and I cannot thank him enough. I was lost for so long and now I'm stronger, less afraid and now live my life again with purpose instead of just existing. A true gift." – *Annie*

"I am still feeling blissful after a glorious session with Jarred. I went to him to get relief from emotional pain as well as physical pain; to my surprise he was this amazing down to earth person who really made me feel relaxed, calm and confident that I chose him to help me. It was amazing how I went from being in severe pain to walking out almost dizzy with joy. Even with my eyes closed I could actually feel his energy pass over me, even face down on a massage table I could feel his presence. He took his time and allowed me the time I needed to analyze each chakra - what each one stood for and how to release the pain I was holding. Many tears were shed but the overwhelming peace and serenity I felt was…out of this world.

"Even when the hot stones were implemented, they literally felt like they melted into my skin like an ice cube on hot pavement. My back pain, which had been restricting me from living in harmony, was relieved. For the first time in over seven years I feel calm, pain free and free from fear, anger, loss, self-blame, shame and most of all, regret. I left all my pain in that room. I feel so calm and so peaceful. This was a very good experience and I am ready to face a new chapter in my life. I feel blessed." - *Tina Anne*

"Another amazing evening, was very soothing to have one of my best friends come through with such detail!" - *Karen*

"Thank-you Jarred, excellent reading, confirmed my intuition." - *Debbie*

"Thank you Jarred - got the answers I was looking for." - *Bonnie*

"Jarred was amazing. His gift is genuine. Every second of his readings makes you want to hear more. There were many things he brought to my attention that he could not possibly have known prior to our appointment. He is worth every penny. Thank you for sharing your very special gift with me and others." – *Anne-Marie*

"Thank you Jarred. Our first session gave me positive vibes. I'm sure I will see you again soon. Your great manners and professional attitude didn't go unnoticed. I would absolutely recommend you. Thank you for your kindness and your help."
- *Agi*

"Thank you - I almost danced like Fred Astaire all the way back to my car...I felt happy and strong. Like a new me. I got home and cleaned out my closet! Like the energizer bunny. I thought I'd be crying but no. I couldn't get to bed until 2 a.m. Wide awake. I woke often during the night as well, but woke up fresh and not tired." - *Charlotte*

"Jarred, I want to tell you the difference you made for me. Since your treatment I am a different me. I was actually able to sleep for the first time in weeks. Furthermore I am used to crying most of the day and almost the entire night. As soon as the tears started rolling, thoughts of you came into my mind and I literally felt lifted up spiritually and felt as if I was surrounded by light and being looked after. Each and every time the tears started they immediately dried up and stopped coming. It was a miracle. I know you deal with angels and holy spirits and I have felt your energy and intense power but this was at another level. I felt as if you and the Angels were there with me protecting me and keeping the tears away and at the same time lifting me up emotionally and spiritually. Thank you. I owe you and can never give you enough to compensate for what you have done for me. You are worth much more than any dollar amount. How can we put a price on a man who does miracles and works with angels? I know you are a humble man and that you get pleasure out of helping others. That being said you deserve everything the world has to offer. Thank you again. BTW I have a friend who will come see you. She lives in the States and is about a six hour plane ride away. Word of you is spreading."
- *Agnus*

"By far the greatest experience I have ever had! I'm so glad I finally came to see you Jarred." - *Mary*

"Hi Jarred - good news! He truly is 100% demon-free. There is continued daily improvement. Unbelievable! Absolutely no sign of anything demonic! No feeling, no energy, no look or behaviours! The crazy episodes that lasted hours and hours and day and night are gone. The demonic behaviour that I can describe as bizarre, violent and the out of control rages are gone! It has been replaced with a normal bad mood or grumpy comment at worst! We are enjoying days of laughing all the time. He is eating well and feeling much better. We are having lots of family outings; family fun and even took a mini dream trip! This is all thanks to you and the incredible work that you do! Thank you for sharing your gift with the world and for healing God's children. God bless you!" - *Laura*

"I feel the difference, Jarred. Your chakra treatment was wonderful. I felt my heart beating in all four stones on my back and today I feel like new. Thank you. Your psychic reading also gave me a lot to think about." - *Maxime*

"Your reading was spot on. Exact. You said exactly what I have felt and what I thought to be true. I could not ask for a better reading, Jarred." - *Lee*

HEAVEN'S MESSENGER

"The other night I met up with a friend, Jarred. I really went with little expectation. Jarred asked to see a picture of my late husband which I gladly showed him. He put his hand over the picture and I was able to feel the energy. He explained to me certain things about talking to the deceased and he started. He described my husband to a "T", he answered a couple of questions for Ricardo that I needed to know. My husband spoke through him! Not like you see in the movies or others who claim they can do this. This was genuine. Everything he told me only I or my kids could have known – private details. I watched him as his eyes were closed the whole time become very emotional as my husband relayed messages he wanted me to know. I am more at peace now and even though I will never get over the loss of my husband, at least I have some closure now. As well the spiritual treatment he did was an incredible experience. I don't know how to describe it to you but I will say when he put his hand over me (not touching me at all) I was able to feel the electricity coming from his hand. As my chakras were closing I was able to feel my whole back vibrate. I am happier, more energetic and my mind seems to be a little clearer. Before I left we also got into a very interesting discussion. His knowledge on the spiritual world is incredible. I learned so much from him. Thank you for everything and I look forward to seeing you again. God Bless." - *Jodi*

"I had the privilege to meet with Jarred following a lot of issues I had to deal with and face up...my energy was very low and I was feeling like there was no light at the end of the tunnel. A few years ago, I was in two relationships with guys who did me a lot of harm and used black magic to take away the nice things planned for me, my pride and my self-worth. Fortunately, Jarred came onto my path and helped me with shamanic treatments and other treatments to remove negative entities from me and he came to my home where some bad entities were affecting the peace and serenity of my house. He got rid of them. Since then, I've been recuperating my energy and have a peaceful home. I referred a friend to Jarred who had similar issues at his house and had spiritual attachments like me. He feels much better now. I feel very fortunate to have met Jarred! He's a very genuine, powerful and generous human being. But, to me, he is also a friend! Thank you so much Jarred for being there." - *Amanda*

"Thank you Jarred. I have grown to feel very comfortable with you and I enjoy our sessions very much. You give me great peace and advice. I am so deeply affected by the communications you share with me, from Gloria, you have no idea. Again, thanks and regards and much love to you and your family." - *Terry*

"If you need to recharge your life batteries, give my friend Jarred a call, or check out services on his web page. Spread the love." - *Joe*

"You're the real deal Jarred...continue this wonderful work! Have a blessed day." - *Tracy*

"Jarred blew my mind on three different occasions. He healed my girlfriend in pain 12 years in three visits. I've sent 43 people to Jarred. 97% were happy!" - *Tony*

"You were really accurate when I met you to contact a deceased person. I was quite the skeptic before, but not anymore. You don't have to convince me! I know you have a special gift. You definitely are the real deal." - *Anne*

"My session with Jarred was incredible! Everything he said was spot on and it was very emotional and healing at the same time! Highly recommend Jarred! Thank you so much again!" - *Tania*

"I had been fighting with my computer for quite a long time now, which is placed in a particular room of the house. This computer would not start as it should; it would crash unexpectedly; opening a new tab or logging on to my e-mail account was always a challenge and seemed to require my begging and a prayer just for me to be able to get an e-mail out. Every day the same scenario repeated itself, even though updates were made - no viruses found - and hard-drive replaced. This morning, after Jarred's cleansing of this room, my computer went on without a hitch! No begging, no wondering, no waiting for the computer to at least start up. Miraculous. Thank you, Jarred!" - *Diane*

"Jarred, after over 2 years of not being able to sell my condo even at under market value, I am happy to say that now, only 3 weeks after you cleansed my condo of entities, we have sold it! Thank you so much!" - *Kim*

"You are gifted by God and God bless you and protect you always for the amazing job you do which is hard work." - *Angela*

"Yay Jarred! I went to see him! Very amazing experience!" - *Shirley*

"Thank you Jarred! I am so grateful for our session at the beginning of the week. I'm remembering my dad today with joy and happiness. I'll always miss him but I know his values and qualities live on!" - Laura

"I've heard of you from others on Facebook and my sister saw you this morning and said how great you are. Thank you. She called me crying and kept saying how incredible you are and about my grandfather and daughter. She made me cry." - *Teresa*

"I have always believed in this stuff. I know what stigmata is. I can't believe I am actually looking at stigmata in action...I can't believe I have witnessed this with my own eyes! It is so clear what I see. Wow. What a blessing and gift you have...I also understand it comes with a great burden and sacrifice." – *David*

"You were mind blowing!" - *Julie*

"I will say one thing: I saw something like this 20 years ago and it was out of this world. Yesterday was brutal and I know the victim over 30 years and he has not been himself to say it nicely. For those who do not believe it, I gain nothing from lying. I only wish it never happens to you. Jarred, I knew you were good last year but after yesterday a lot of people would have left running. The spitting and coughing were unreal. I am still in a cloud. The world we live in." - *Paul*

"Jarred saved my daughter. Most people said it was just her being a teenager but I knew it wasn't her at all. And even to those who don't believe, my daughter went from being silent and angry with evil stares to laughing and smiling when we left. Whether you believe or not, if you think there is something wrong with someone you know, it's worth taking them to Jarred to make sure. I'm so thankful I know this amazing man." - *Isabelle*

"You are the real deal." - *Maureen*

"Had a very interesting experience during a reading with Jarred. He was telling me about his stigmata, and talking with his hands (Jarred's way). I stopped him to ask him to hold up his hands for me. This confirmed what I was seeing...a glowing light in the centre of his palms!

"Weird? Yup, but I did see it so thought I would share. Go see him for a reading and maybe you will too! He is terrific!" - *Melissa*

"Jarred operates at a higher frequency. He has raised his vibration to such a point that he can use his palm chakras to heal, or repel evil. Love this guy. Glad he's in our community." – *Don*

"Jarred was able to answer a lot of questions for me based on what he saw. He was able to provide the guidance. He gave me the confidence I lacked to make the correct decisions I needed to make. He was professional and accurate." – *Andrew*

"I went to see Jarred mainly to communicate with a deceased relative and very close friend who passed on. The description of them and things they told Jarred were so accurate. Even down to the movement of the mouth and sounds made by my good friend after drinking the whiskey he so loved to drink! Jarred made me feel comfortable the entire time I was there." - *Lisa*

REFERENCES:

1. Rachel Ray, Leading US exorcists explain huge increase in demand for the Rite – and priests to carry them out, http://www.telegraph.co.uk/news/2016/09/26/leading-us-exorcists-explain-huge-increase-in-demand-for-the-rit/
Accessed November 2017.

2. Irish priest asks for back-up as demand for exorcisms rises 'exponentially'
www.catholicnewsagency.com
Accessed January 2018

3. Psychiatrist claims: The Cause of Mental Illness is Demonic Possession, https://www.disclose.tv/psychiatrist-claims-the-cause-of-mental-illness-is-demonic-possession-313688
Accessed December 2017

4. Top Psychiatrist: Demonic Possession is Very Real and On the Rise – CBN News, https://www1.cbn.com/cbnnews/2016/july/top-psychiatrist-demonic-possession-is-very-real-and-on-the-rise
Accessed December 2017

ABOUT THE AUTHOR

Jarred Neil resides in the beautiful town of St-Lazare, Quebec with his wife and five children. If you would like to reach out to him, you can visit his website at www.jarredheavensmessenger.com.

Currently, Jarred is working on multiple projects.

Look for Jarred in the movie *The Lodge*, scheduled for release in November 2018.

www.ingramcontent.com/pod-product-compliance
Lightning Source LLC
Chambersburg PA
CBHW022132080426
42734CB00006B/323